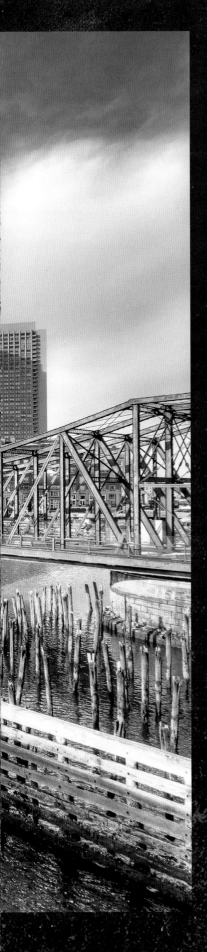

The Boston Homegrown Cookbook

Local Food, Local Restaurants, Local Recipes

By Leigh Belanger
Photography by Margaret Belanger

Voyageur Press

Contents

Summer

Fall

Winter

Foreword

Fiore di Nonno's Lourdes Smith first began making her artisan mozzarella cheese in the Nuestra Culinary Kitchen in Jamaica Plain. She sold it to restaurants in town—Oleana, Craigie on Main, and others—and the chefs identified Smith's cheese on their menus. Soon, you could buy the cheese at the Copley farmers' market and at Formaggio Kitchen. Today, Smith's line of cheeses is scattered on menus and in retail markets across town.

Smith's is just one of Boston's recent local food success stories. As restaurants have started identifying farms, cheese makers, and fishermen on their menus, consumer recognition and demand has grown. Retail stores have done the same, purchasing more local products and highlighting producers in their displays. Awareness of Boston's local food community—whether artisans, farmers, purveyors, or chefs—has never been higher.

It hasn't always been this way. Coming to the Boston area from New York City in the early 1980s sent me immediately into a coma of food withdrawal. At the time, Boston had its own food culture—lobster, clam chowder, and the North End's traditional Italian favorites (spaghetti with red sauce, pizza)—but nothing like what was happening in New York.

True ethnic restaurants were making an appearance in Cambridge: Joyce Chen's Chinese cuisine, Spanish at Café Pamplona, and Casablanca's Mediterranean offerings. And restaurants were opening that had a new flair to their menus, with more "gourmet" spins on traditional dishes. Jasper's, opened by Jasper White, was one of the first seafood restaurants to move away from boiled lobsters, fried clams, and chowder to dishes like his signature pan-roasted lobster. Figs, a small storefront restaurant in Charlestown, served gourmet pizzas (figs, prosciutto, and gorgonzola to name just one) that were a huge departure from traditional cheese pizza. But in New England tradition, the food was still mostly derived from what was respected and accepted in the area.

As a consumer, I was thrilled with all the new restaurants. But what about home cooking? I could find good meat at Savenor's in Boston and gourmet specialty items at Formaggio Kitchen in Cambridge, but finding locally grown and produced ingredients still was a scavenger hunt. To this day, I remember how excited I was to find an Iggy's ficelle.

It wasn't until the late 1980s and early 1990s that things started to change. Slowly, new outlets opened up. Small roadside farm stands grew into full-scale markets offering milk, bread, baked goods, jams, and other specialty products along with their own produce. Consumer demand helped establish Wilson Farms, Verrill Farms, Allandale Farm, and Idylwilde Farm, to name a few. Today, with more than four hundred throughout the state, farm stands play an important role in our food community.

Farmers' markets were also important in the development of Boston's local food movement. In the late 1970s there were maybe 70 markets around the state. Today there are more than 220. The perfect venue for startup artisan food companies, farmers' markets enable producers to get their products into the market without a large initial overhead expense. Farmers' market organizers also found that having an assortment of products, from produce to chocolate sauce, enhanced the markets and increased sales for all involved. Many of our favorite artisan food products—Westfield Farm goat cheese, Iggy's bread, Taza chocolate—were first sampled and available at the farmers' markets.

As the movement evolved and expanded, so did the seasons for farmers' markets and farm stands. No longer an April–November business, markets and stands are extending their seasons, and farms are doing more winter growing. In 2011, Massachusetts was home to more than twelve winter farmers' markets, all a success for both the producers and the consumers. New community kitchens are opening up, allowing more small producers to get started.

Today the demand for local products is even stronger. Consumers are questioning where their food comes from and understand that supporting local businesses helps the community as a whole. Local food has become a major part of the food culture. While there are still hurdles—price, accessibility, production, and distribution—consumer demand is so strong that problems are being worked out.

From artisan producers and retailers to the chefs, restaurant owners, farmers, and other suppliers profiled in this book, a strong local food community is now well-established in Boston, and the success is a win for everyone.

—by Ilene Bezhaler, Editor, *Edible Boston*

Introduction

Growing up south of Boston in the 1980s, I ate like any normal kid with two working parents: frozen pizza, chicken a la king, and the occasional (and highly anticipated) trip to Burger King. My mom cooked to feed us, not to express herself. Unless it was a holiday, food was "no-fuss." Sometimes, though, it was central to a special occasion—like when we ate corn on the cob and boiled lobster for my dad's birthday in August.

These two stalwarts of seasonal New England feasting didn't make many appearances in our household. They required big pots and were messy to prepare, eat, and clean up. My father always ate an enormous amount of corn, piling on the butter and methodically devouring the kernels, left to right, like a typewriter. He attacked the lobster with similar gusto, sucking the meat out of every little leg and saving the tail for last. Hands covered in butter, corn silk in my teeth, empty red exoskeletons and corn cobs piled on the table, I loved these meals but hated when they ended, since it would be another year before we'd have lobster again.

I didn't think of it this way, but the annual lobster feasts were the most explicit seasonal eating I did growing up. I had no idea about local food until I moved to Washington for college in the late 1990s. A permanent farmers' market in town housed dozens of stalls for nearby organic farmers growing produce and fruit—cherries and apples and berries of all kinds, along with fresh or smoked king salmon and oysters and clams dug from flats just outside town and sold fresh in sacks or shucked, on ice, to eat right there. My friends and I joined a community supported agriculture farm (CSA) and planted a garden. I took seasonal work on a nearby farm. I worked as a line cook in a restaurant serving Pacific Northwest cuisine.

This new world transformed the way I thought about food. I started cooking seasonally for myself and my friends, and anticipating the ways the dishes and meals would change with the weather and the crops. It made so much sense, in such a satisfying way. Little did I know it, but back on the East Coast, Boston's farm-to-table community was burgeoning, and had been since I was a kid, eyeing the lobster pot.

In the early 1980s, a book like this wouldn't have been possible. New American Cuisine was dawning, but "you couldn't find a New England apple in the Star Market," says Jasper White, one of the first chefs in Boston to track down local producers and build his menus around their ingredients. When White was first cooking, the exciting restaurants were in hotels, and the model was French. The food was exquisite, but it wasn't local. And there were few other destinations for a memorable meal, as there are today.

As Boston's restaurant scene matured alongside American food culture in general, chef-driven restaurants popped up—and these chefs, like Gordon Hamersley, Steve Johnson, and Jody Adams, were early supporters of local suppliers. "In the old days," says Hamersley, "we had to go out and find the farmers. But over time they got a lot more organized."

spring

Just when seasonal eating has challenged your love for stored root crops, peppery greens, and astringent rhubarb arrive to wake up your palate. And even though the season's wind and rain can be unforgiving, when the warm weather does roll in, so do the weeks of eating asparagus with every meal, the flats of strawberries for the year's first preserving projects, and the exuberant menus from chefs who have been waiting to work with the season's bright, bracing flavors.

Summer Shack

Chef Jasper White

Verrill Farm

It's hard to pinpoint when Boston became a great eating town, but some of the action happened in the Bostonian Hotel in the 1980s. Jasper White, cooking with his friend Lydia Shire, was combining precise cooking technique with ingredients sourced from coastal New England. For decades, serious food in the United States had been French food, but in the early 1980s American chefs were starting to come into their own. When offered the chef position at the Bostonian, White said he'd take the job if he could do an American menu.

White, who dropped out of college to become a cook, later graduated from the Culinary Institute of America in Hyde Park, New York. He was raised on a farm near the Jersey Shore, with an Italian grandmother who set a high standard for cooking, he says. An immigrant who adapted to life in the United States by maintaining her habits of seasonal cooking and eating, White's grandmother was his biggest influence. His childhood experiences with food—eating what the family grew in their garden, caught at the seashore, and hunted—shaped his approach to cooking.

That influence stuck with White when he became a professional cook. "Once I mastered the techniques," says White, "I started thinking about how I could bring in my own food. A lot of my style has to do with the way I view food and ingredients. If I lived in Hawaii, I'd be a Hawaiian chef. Arizona, same thing." But White made Boston his home.

As his ingredient-based style of cooking evolved, White took a broad view of what constituted New England food. "I didn't base it strictly on traditions," he says. He discovered great ingredients in parts of the state with large Portuguese populations, stumbled onto apple orchards in central Massachusetts, drove to Milton for herbs, and brought the ingredients back first to the Bostonian and later to his own restaurant, Jasper's, which opened in 1983 on the waterfront downtown.

After closing Jasper's in the mid-1990s, White opened the Summer Shack in Cambridge, a casual, family-friendly restaurant inspired by coastal New England seafood joints. "I was at the point where I felt like I'd done what I could do with fine dining. I wanted to do simple, casual food—and show that it could still be high-quality," he says.

White was one of the first fine-dining chefs in the area to turn his talents to a casual restaurant, a trend that has transformed the city's dining landscape.

"I moved here in 1979," says White. "At the time, you couldn't buy a New England apple at the Star Market."

"I cannot describe what's happened in the last thirty years," he continues. "I've watched the whole thing evolve from nothing to something pretty special."

One of the first farms White worked with remains, more than twenty years later, an important source for restaurants. Concord's

two-hundred-acre Verrill Farm began selling to chefs in the early 1990s, after the family's final herd of dairy cows was sold and the farm transitioned to growing produce and running a farm stand.

Verrill Farm began as a dairy farm in 1922, started by current owner Steve Verrill's father. Steve took over the farm in 1957 after graduating from Cornell University and maintained the dairy cows through many volatile years in the industry, finally selling the herd in 1990. "It was a tough business physically and financially," says Verrill. By focusing on produce, the family could have more control over their pricing, he says.

At first the Verrills focused on pick-your-own and farmers' markets—the farm's restaurant wholesale evolved from there. As the Verrills built their business, the family stopped selling at farmers' markets and focused on restaurants and chefs instead. Today, the farm sells to more than thirty restaurants.

"The chefs have certainly had a role in our evolution," says Verrill. Having his name on restaurant menus throughout the city has helped bring business to the farm itself—which, with its pick-your-own fields, pie-eating contests, and seasonal festivals, draws crowds from all over Greater Boston.

Working with the chefs has also helped Verrill Farm expand its retail offerings. Before the chefs discovered heirloom tomatoes, says Verrill, they didn't budge off the shelves. "Now that they're big in the restaurants," he says, "they're the most popular thing at the farm stand." Same for less common produce, he continues. "I'd never heard of celeriac before a chef asked me to grow it."

Baby Lamb Kidneys with Morels

From Jasper White's *Cooking from New England* (Harper Perennial, 1989)

Serves 2 as an appetizer

The scaled-down landscape of New England is particularly appropriate for the farming of smaller animals, and lamb and goat are very well-suited to the terrain. Kidneys from a mature lamb are somewhat of an acquired taste, but those of baby lamb are quite mildly flavored. You can substitute veal kidneys if you wish.

2 baby lamb kidneys
salt and freshly ground black pepper
1 tbsp. clarified butter
2 medium shallots, finely chopped
1/2 c. morel mushrooms, thickly sliced
2 tbsp. good cognac or other good brandy
1 tsp. Dijon mustard
2 tbsp. veal stock, reduced
2 tbsp. heavy cream
1 tbsp. chives, freshly chopped
2 thick slices baguette, lightly buttered and toasted

Split the kidneys in half lengthwise and trim off any fat. Season lightly with salt and pepper. Heat the clarified butter in a small sauté pan. Add the kidneys and quickly brown on both sides; remove from pan and put on a small plate.

Add the shallots and morels to the pan and sauté for 1 minute. Then add the cognac or brandy and ignite. When the flame has burned off, add the mustard, stock, and heavy cream; reduce until thick enough to coat a spoon. Return the kidneys to the sauce; add the chives and cook for another 30 seconds.

Arrange the kidneys and morels on small appetizer plates or in tartlet shells and spoon the sauce over. If serving toast, place it on the corner of the plate (it will be needed for extra sauce). Serve immediately.

* For a variation, add four cooked asparagus tips to the sauce right before the kidneys.

Fettuccine with Lobster and Fresh Peas or Asparagus

From Lobster at Home (Scribner, 1998)

Serves 4 as a first course or 2 as a hearty main course

Peas love cool climates and are very easy to grow in New England. In late spring they are so plentiful that they are available at almost every market and roadside stand. You can also use fresh asparagus for this recipe. Late spring is a great time for lobsters too; after the cold winter waters begin to warm up, they feed voraciously and are full of sweet, tender meat.

2 live 1–1 1/4-lb. hard-shell lobsters

kosher or sea salt

1 lb. fresh garden peas (or 8 oz. fresh asparagus)

8 oz. dried fettuccine

2 tbsp. olive oil

freshly ground pepper

2 tbsp. unsalted butter

2 tbsp. fresh chives, finely minced

2 tbsp. Parmigiano-Reggiano cheese, grated

Fill a large (10–12-qt.) pot with water. Add enough salt to make it taste like ocean water. When the pot comes to a rolling boil, submerge the lobsters and parboil for 3 minutes. Drain and let cool at room temperature. Use a cleaver to crack and remove the meat from the claws, knuckles, and tails. Remove the cartilage from the claws and the intestine from the tail. Cut the lobster meat into a 3/4-inch dice. Cover and refrigerate. You have the option of either cracking open and picking the carcass for meat to be added to the diced meat or reserving it to make soup.

Shuck the peas (you should have about 1 c.). Blanch them in boiling salted water for about 1 minute until tender. Remove the peas from the boiling water and submerge in ice water immediately to stop the cooking. Drain and reserve. If using asparagus, peel the stalks (unless they are small and tender "pencils") and cut on the diagonal into 3/4-inch pieces. Blanch in boiling water for 1–2 minutes until tender. Remove the asparagus from the boiling water and submerge in ice water immediately to stop the cooking. Drain and reserve.

Fill a 6- to 8-qt. pot with 4 qt. water and add 4 tbsp. salt. Bring to a rolling boil. Before you add the fettuccine, organize the other ingredients. There will be no time to spare once you start cooking the pasta. Heat a large sauté pan (10 inches) over medium heat. Add the fettuccine to the boiling water. It will take 6–8 minutes to cook.

After the pasta has been cooking for 2 minutes, add the olive oil and the diced lobster meat to the sauté pan. It should be sizzling. Grind a little pepper over the lobster and sauté for about 2 minutes, turning the pieces with tongs. The oil will turn red. Add the peas or asparagus; lower the heat and sauté for 1 minute more.

Drain the pasta in a colander thoroughly so that the pasta is as free of water as possible, and add it to the sauté pan. Add the butter and chives. Toss or stir the fettuccine so that it becomes coated with the pan juices. Season lightly with salt and adjust the pepper. Place in a large bowl or divide evenly among warmed bowls. Sprinkle with cheese and serve at once.

Asparagus

The California Asparagus Commission likes to tout asparagus as an "international food." It is grown from China to Poland to the Mediterranean, where it is thought to have originated. The name itself comes from a Greek word for a green shoot, but in one Western Massachusetts town it's known by a different name.

Asparagus's Bay State moniker, **Hadley grass**, ought to give the reader a sense of how important its cultivation once was in Hadley and much of western Massachusetts. Until at least the 1970s, the region's sandy topsoil was thought to produce some of the best asparagus available, and the region's product was prized afar.

When buying asparagus, don't be falsely tempted by the fattest stalks. Spears the width of a swizzle stick may be the most delicious, if they're picked fresh.

Cuisine en Locale

Chef JJ Gonson
Stillman's at the Turkey Farm

A nine-course descent into Hell. A feast in Valhalla, complete with dramatic readings and Viking hats for the guests. Oh, and weekly shares of from-scratch local food, delivered to your home if you want. This is the work of JJ Gonson, a self-described locavore chef whose personal chef and catering business, Cuisine en Locale, is about feeding people local food—and throwing in some theater while she's at it.

Trained as an art teacher with a background in fine art photography and photojournalism, Gonson has always cooked. When she was pregnant with her first child, now ten, she began reading about milk, and her concern about conventional production methods turned her into a food activist. "I said to myself, we're feeding toxins to children," she explains. "What's the solution?"

For Gonson, the solution was to buy food from people she knew and trusted—local farmers. Cuisine en Locale spun out of her desire to share that experience with others.

Because her business is based on local food (she buys food from places in Pennsylvania to Maine but sticks to Massachusetts as much as possible), Gonson spends a good portion of her time sourcing and preserving ingredients. Her chest freezer is filled with local meat, and she does a lot of dehydrating and canning—in 2010 she put up 40 quarts of tomatoes. "My favorite farmer quote," she says, "is 'in New England we spend six months getting ready for winter and six months getting ready for summer.' It feels that way sometimes."

In the process, Gonson has built strong relationships with many farms in the area. She works closely with Kate Stillman, who raises livestock in Hardwick, west of Boston in central Massachusetts. "We really do have a partnership," says Gonson. The two met at a farmers' market where Stillman sells her beef, pork, lamb, and chicken.

"I've never had a relationship like this with any other chef," says Stillman. She grew up working markets with her parents, whose Stillman Farms in New Braintree sells fruit and vegetables at farmers' markets around the city, and has worked with many of the chefs in town. In terms of buying local, Stillman says about Gonson, "I don't know anyone who pushes it to the level she does."

Stillman started raising livestock after college. She knew she wanted to get into farming on her own, and she found a farm in Hardwick that was set up for animals, with barns and fencing in place. Although her experience with animals was limited, she saw that there was a demand that needed to be met—and raising livestock also allowed her to create a niche apart from her parents' farm.

Working directly with a chef like Gonson is more the exception than the rule for Stillman, whose main focus is on farmers' markets and CSAs. "Some farms handle it better, but we like to keep things diverse," says Stillman. "And the markets work really well for us—we've become quite efficient at packing up the truck and driving the two hours to Boston." The chefs she does work with are often those whose restaurants are near the markets where the family has their stalls, like Sel de la Terre in the Back Bay near the Copley market, or Centre St. Café in Jamaica Plain, where the Stillmans do a market on Saturdays.

But with Gonson, the relationship has evolved into a friendship between two businesswomen and mothers who support and promote each other whenever they can. There are few, if any, other clients from whom Stillman would take calls and orders in the middle of the night, but, says the farmer, "I'm willing to do almost anything to facilitate the work with her."

BBQ Pork Ribs

This recipe is for 4 to 6 full racks, which serves somewhere between 12 and 18 people.
Feel free to reduce it or expand it to meet your needs.

1 gal. apple cider or organic white grape juice

2 c. plum wine or other sweet wine

1 c. salt

1 c. sugar

1/4 c. whole star anise

2 tbsp. whole allspice

1 whole Sichuan pepper

1 tbsp. other peppercorns

1 large knob fresh ginger (about the size of an adult thumb)

4–6 full racks of pork ribs

1 c. maple sugar or brown sugar

1 tbsp. dry oregano

2 tbsp. paprika

1 tbsp. powdered chili

1 c. boiled apple cider

Bring the cider, wine, salt, sugar, anise, allspice, pepper, and ginger to a boil in a large pot. Boil the liquid for 10 minutes, and while it is boiling, fill the sink halfway with ice water. Turn off the heat and place the pot in the sink of ice water to cool down the brine. Submerge the pork ribs, and refrigerate for at least 24 hours (48 hours is better). You can do this in any vessel in which they can be completely under the liquid—from a baggie to a big bucket.

Drain, reserve the brining liquid (don't throw it away!), and pick off the bits of spices that might cling to the meat. Pat the meat dry. Strain the brining liquid into a sauce pan, and put it back on the stove, bringing it to a full boil for at least 10 minutes to kill any bacteria from the pork. Keep it hot, and remove any scum that forms on the top. Heat the oven to 250 degrees. Combine the sugar, oregano, paprika, and chili powder in a small bowl, then rub over the ribs. Place the ribs as separately as possible on baking sheets (unless you have rib racks) in the oven for as long as it takes to roast them to a delicious caramel brown color (about 5 hours). Turn them every half hour and rotate as necessary for even cooking. Whenever you move them, baste them liberally with the boiled brining liquid and pan drippings. (Roasting meat is a sponge; if you keep putting liquid on it, the result will be nice and moist, not dried out.)

When the ribs are all well cooked, pile them carefully in braising pans, add enough brining liquid to cover the bottom of the pan, and cover them tightly with foil. Increase the oven temperature to 300 degrees. Return the ribs to the oven, and allow them to continue to braise for at least another hour, or until they are moist and falling off the bone in places.

Mix one part boiled brining liquid with one part boiled cider (or pomegranate molasses) and brush ribs all over. At this point you can cool them to save for later or even freeze them once they are cold, but of course they are best right away! When you are ready to serve them, heat them over a grill or covered in the oven, topped with more heated sauce. Bon appétit!

BBQ Pork Ribs

Pork

It is almost as though the good food movement rode in on a Large Black pig, the way pork has become beloved by cooks and eaters everywhere. But what's not to love about so generous an animal—one that gives "everything but the squeal" to the cause of the culinary arts? Whether it's braised shoulder, smoked ribs, fresh or cured sausage, roasted loin, fried chops—or, of course, bacon—there's no other animal that delivers quite like the pig. Pork from animals raised on mixed-crop farms is often available to consumers at farmers' markets or through CSAs. These pigs, which have grown more slowly and have eaten a more diverse diet than those raised in confinement, are also often bred for their flavor profiles. It's pork worth seeking out—the better the pig, the better the bacon.

Wheat Berry Pilaf

Serves 4 as a side dish

3 c. water
1 c. wheat berries, uncooked
1 tbsp. plus 1 tsp. canola or sunflower oil
1 medium white onion, diced into 1/2-inch pieces
1 clove garlic, chopped
2 carrots, diced into 1/2-inch pieces
chili powder and salt to taste
1 small bunch of Swiss chard, stems and ribs removed
2 tbsp. paprika
1 c. pinto beans, cooked
salt and pepper to taste

Bring water to a boil. Add the wheat berries, reduce heat to a simmer, and cook for 45 minutes or until the grain is just soft. Drain and transfer to a large mixing bowl.

Heat 1 tbsp. of the oil in a large skillet. Add the onion and cook over medium heat for 5 minutes until soft and translucent. Add the garlic and cook until soft. Increase the heat to medium-high, add the carrots, and cook, stirring constantly, for about 10 minutes, until the pieces are browned and soft to the bite. Season in the pan with chili powder and salt. Tip the contents of the skillet into the mixing bowl with the wheat berries and wipe the skillet clean.

Heat the remaining oil in the skillet over medium heat. Add the chard and cook until wilted and reduced to less than half its original volume. Season with salt and add to mixing bowl. Add the beans to the bowl. Gently mix the contents of the bowl together, adjust the seasoning to taste, and serve. Can be served warm, cold, or at room temperature.

Lineage,
Island Creek Oyster Bar

Chef Jeremy Sewall and Pastry Chef Lisa Sewall
Island Creek Oysters

Jeremy Sewall, Lineage owner and Island Creek Oyster Bar partner, has an ingredient network most chefs would kill for. For both restaurants, lobsters come down fresh from his cousin's boat in York, Maine, and his business partner at Island Creek brings oysters fresh from the flats in Duxbury, south of Boston. "There are days when I pinch myself," says the chef.

Sewall grew up among commercial fishermen in southern Maine, "eating out of huge family gardens," he remembers. "Growing our own food was a matter of necessity." When Sewall was a teenager, his father urged him to find a skill he could master and build a career on. "It wasn't like I had some big epiphany" about becoming a chef, he says, "but I liked food and cooking, so it made sense."

Sewall, now thirty-eight, attended the Culinary Institute of America and was fortunate to head to California to work at a time when the farm-to-table restaurant scene was bursting. "Being a young cook and chef in California, where 80 percent of the produce was farm direct all year," he says, "you could do it well." This approach, though more difficult in New England, has influenced Sewall's work from early in his career. "I still go to the farmers' market in Coolidge Corner with the staff," he says, to build what he calls his "ingredient-driven" style of food.

Lineage, which Sewall co-owns with his wife, Lisa, a pastry chef, turned five in 2010, and now it has a sibling, the Island Creek Oyster Bar. ICOB for short, this restaurant is a far different creature than sophisticated mom-and-pop spot Lineage. It's big, sexy, and in a swank hotel near Fenway Park. But it's not new to Sewall, who operated a different seafood restaurant in the same space years ago.

This time around, Sewall partnered with power-restaurateur Garrett Harker and Island Creek Oysters owner Skip Bennett to open the urbane fish joint serving seafood Sewall says is so fresh, they need to wait for it to come out of rigor mortis to properly butcher it. "The look on some of the sous-chefs' faces" when they get to work with fish that fresh, he says, "is priceless."

Down in Duxbury, Sewall's partner Skip Bennett oversees the crew at Island Creek Oysters. At the tip of a spiffy pier jutting into Duxbury Bay on the South Shore of Boston is the Oysterplex, a tiny shack and the hub of Island Creek's fast-expanding oyster farm and wholesale operation. Two young men stand over a tall central table, sizing and counting oysters pulled from the waters beyond the pier and piling them into mesh bags. Most of the bags are headed to Boston to fill orders for restaurants across town, including ICOB in Kenmore Square.

Shellfish aquaculture is relatively new in Massachusetts, and Bennett was an early pioneer, starting his business in the mid-1990s. He grew up in seaside Duxbury and, after earning a finance degree in college, turned his business know-how to making a living on the

water. He didn't want to be a commercial fisherman, though—"Too inconsistent," he says. He gave aquaculture a go, and after a batch of clams got wiped out by a parasite, he turned his attention to oysters.

Once seen mostly in fine dining restaurants, raw bars have proliferated on all sorts of menus in the years since Bennett has been in business. Working with chefs is not without its challenges, admits Bennett, but the payoff is being able to do business with passionate people who can spread the word about Island Creek. "If you can win over great chefs," he says, "others will be willing to give it a try." So far, so good.

Chilled Maine Lobster
with Blood Orange Vinaigrette and English Peas

Serves 4

This is a great dish that straddles the seasons: the beginning of spring when the first peas just start and the blood oranges are in their final weeks creates this great combination of flavors.

3 blood oranges
2 sprigs fresh thyme, leaves removed and stems saved
1/2 c. shelled English peas, blanched and shocked
2 1 1/4-lb. lobsters, cooked, cooled, and meat removed
1/2 c. pea greens (if not available, use arugula)
3 tbsp. Marcona almonds, lightly toasted
1 tbsp. lemon juice
2 tbsp. extra virgin olive oil
salt and pepper to taste

With a sharp knife, remove the skin from the blood oranges and cut into sections. Save all the juice from the oranges and squeeze any extra juice from the pith into a small saucepan. Place the thyme stems in the juice and reduce slowly until the juice begins to thicken; remove and discard stems. Remove from heat and let cool to room temperature.

Peel the peas so only the tender center of the pea remains. Toss the lobster, pea greens, peas, and almonds in a mixing bowl. Add the lemon juice, olive oil, salt, and pepper and toss until well coated but not dripping.

Arrange each plate with half a lobster, peas, greens, and almonds. Divide the orange sections among each plate; sprinkle with thyme leaves, salt, and pepper. Drizzle the orange reduction around the plate and serve at once.

Island Creek Oysters
with Rosé Mignonette

For about 24 oysters

This is a very simple but very satisfying way to eat oysters. If you don't have rosé, any good white sparkling or still wine will work.

- **24 Island Creek oysters**
- **1 large shallot, peeled and minced**
- **1 tsp. cracked black pepper**
- **1/2 c. sparkling rosé wine**
- **1/4 c. Champagne vinegar**

Shuck the oysters and place on a bed of ice. Mix the shallots, pepper, rosé wine, and Champagne vinegar in a small bowl and spoon a small amount of the mignonette on each oyster just before eating.

Oysters

Oysters are as seductive a food to some as they are repellent to others. Luckily, oyster lovers have more outlets than ever to slurp and learn about their favorite bivalves. In many ways, oysters hold the promise of an improved food system: they reflect their origins; they can be farmed easily and in abundance (although they are also caught in the wild); and they are a low-cost protein whose cultivation has proven ecological benefits. In other words, they are sustainable and, for many people, delicious. Between their diet, the tides, the water temperature, and the surrounding habitat where they grow, oysters can taste wildly different from one farm or one bay to another, even if those places are near each other.

Tosca

Chef Kevin Long
Weir River Farm

"Seventeen years ago, suburbia was not this interesting," says Kevin Long, who has worked at Tosca in Hingham, a suburb south of Boston, since starting as a prep cook at eighteen years old. With its vaulted ceiling, exposed brick and beams, open kitchen, and big wood-burning oven, Tosca was among the first beautifully designed, chef-driven fine-dining restaurants to open in Boston's suburbs.

That was 1993. Long became Tosca's executive chef in 1999 and has since overseen the back-of-the-house operations at a restaurant that remains an anchor in a much more crowded suburban dining scene.

Growing up in nearby Rockland, Long was the first kid in his family to attend college, but he didn't finish. He was studying computer technology at Bridgewater State, a nearby community college, but "my dad was out of work at the time, and I just had this feeling, like, I gotta get a job and save the family," he explains. While Long was growing up, his father had worked in a restaurant kitchen and "could do a lot of stuff in the kitchen that regular mom-and-dad cooks couldn't do."

Long's first job, washing dishes and working the prep shift at a local spot, piqued his interest in restaurants. He's left Tosca only once in the seventeen years he's worked there, to open a French bistro-style restaurant in Boston's South End in the late 1990s.

Tosca's menu under Long is a kind of seasonal Italian-inspired food for everyone. Steaks and Caesar salads are big in the suburbs—two items that never come off the menu. But cooking seasonally, says Long, "It's everything we do." Whether it means Nantucket Bay scallops in November, Maine shrimp in February, or seasonal produce throughout the year, "Between 25 and 40 percent of our food sales are done in nightly seasonal specials," he continues. For these, he depends on a well-tended network of fish, produce, and meat suppliers.

"There are farmers we've worked with for eight or nine years," he explains. "A lot of them just have a half or a quarter-acre in their backyards." But because many of his suppliers are so small, Tosca is their only client, and Long can ask them to grow precisely what he wants. Same with his lobsters, which come straight off the boat from an old-school lobsterman in Hull, the town next door. "I know the life stories of the suppliers and their families," he says.

"I have to say, working this way, I know it's no secret, but if you buy your Brussels sprouts all trimmed in a little cup it's easier," he says, than facing the extra planning and prep time that accompany his work with tiny local farms. "These growers, you have to give them a little extra love." When legendary Vermont lamb producer Lydia Ratcliff calls, "I buy it even if I don't need it. I just buy it." It's a rare spot for any chef to find himself in, he admits. The suburbs have been kind.

And the kindness keeps coming: a farm recently popped up down the street from Tosca. Once a private estate, Weir River Farm is now a livestock and vegetable farm on Boston's South Shore.

About a decade ago, the former estate was donated to the Trustees of Reservations, a conservation organization that preserves and manages historic and ecologically significant Massachusetts properties.

Well-heeled Hingham is the last place you'd think to find any livestock roaming. But tucked away on hilly, rocky pastures, the Trustees have transitioned the estate into a working farm, and Belted Galloway cattle, Tamworth pigs, chickens, goats, and sheep dot the fields. Along with the livestock, veggies grown on about three-and-a-half acres yield a huge diversity of produce, says grower Amy Baron.

Baron was recruited by the Trustees after apprenticing at another agricultural property in Dover. Weir River Farm has been a welcome addition to the community, she says. "At the farmers' market," Baron says, "people were first coming to us for greens, but they got excited about these specialty things we grew that the other growers didn't, like Harukei turnips, bok choi, and kale." Response at the farmers' market in 2010 was so strong that they put a CSA program in place the following season.

Baron has also reached out to the restaurant community in Hingham, including Tosca and Scarlet Oak Tavern, across town. "My first year, I started late in the season," says Baron. "When I realized we wouldn't have time to get to the farmers' market, I literally asked my supervisor who to call."

Tosca was on the list, and soon enough, "we started working with them week in and week out," with the restaurant using Weir River produce for seasonal specials. Baron hopes to continue the relationship and expand into custom growing for Tosca and other area restaurants, on top of the CSA and the farm's educational programs.

"It's pretty unique where we are in Hingham, since we're one of the only vegetable growers in town," says Baron. "It's nice to be able to sell to restaurants and have people make the connection that they're eating something grown right down the road."

Risotto Verde

Serves 4

3/4 c. garlic scapes, roughly chopped
1 shallot, roughly chopped
2 sprigs thyme
8 black peppercorns, crushed
1/2 red jalapeño pepper, roughly chopped
1 tbsp. butter
3 tbsp. water
1 c. heavy cream
3 tbsp. sugar
1 garlic clove
1 lb. spinach, blanched and dried well
4 tbsp. unsalted butter
1 small onion, diced
1/8 c. white wine
1/8 c. water
1 c. Carnaroli rice
2 handfuls of grated Parmigiano and Piave Vecchio cheeses
(about 1/3 c.—most hard aged cheese will do here)

Combine the garlic scapes, shallot, thyme, peppers, butter, and water in a medium-sized saucepan and wilt on low heat until soft, about 15 minutes. Add the cream, sugar, and garlic clove. Reduce heat to low and cook gently until liquid has reduced to 1 c. Take care not to scorch. Discard garlic. Add the blanched spinach and warm through. Quickly transfer to a high-speed blender and purée until vibrant green and as smooth as possible. Transfer into a clean bowl and set in a larger bowl of ice to set the green color. Season with kosher salt.

In a large saucepan over medium heat, melt the butter. When it foams, add the onion, wine, and water. Cook over medium heat until wilted, about 8–10 minutes. Add the rice and lightly toast on top. Gradually stir in additional water, 2 c. at a time, stirring over medium heat until the rice is tender, about 25 minutes. When the rice is creamy and tender, stir in the green purée and cheese. Warm it through, check seasoning, and serve immediately.

Grilled Lamb with Green Garlic

Serves 4

2 10–12-oz. spring lamb loins, trimmed of excessive fat
1 lb. garlic scapes, long and tender
olive oil
salt and pepper

Prepare a charcoal or wood grill. Once the coals are glowing and the heat is medium-high, add the lamb. Slowly grill the lamb loins until medium-rare, about 8 minutes on each side, basting with olive oil, salt, and black pepper. In the last 5 minutes, nestle the garlic scapes alongside the lamb on the grill.

Remove the lamb from the grill to a cutting board, cover with foil, and let rest for 10 minutes. Slice thinly. Pool the risotto on the bottom of a pre-warmed platter. Layer the sliced lamb on top of the rice. Nestle in the grilled garlic scapes. Drizzle with extra virgin olive oil and serve.

Lamb

Lamb's fatty texture has led to various sauces and herbal rubs designed to cut through its unctuousness. The most well-known is probably mint jelly (as in the pun, "Make like mint jelly and take it on the lam"). It appears in cookbooks as early as 1859 and is probably a variation on the favorite British condiment with lamb, mint sauce, which contains just chopped fresh mint, sugar, and vinegar.

But lamb lovers need not restrict themselves to mint. Mediterranean cuisine often has it cooked in red wine. In North Africa, notes the *Oxford Companion to Food*, apricots or quinces often are combined with lamb in stews. Garlic preparations, such as the one offered here, are typical of French lamb dishes.

L'Espalier

Chef/Owner Frank McLelland
Apple Street Farm

Hauling produce bins in his muck boots and barn jacket, Frank McClelland looks at ease on his way up from the fields at Apple Street Farm. McClelland's first year as a farmer was 2009. With fourteen acres in vegetable production as of 2011, the farm sells most of its produce to the restaurants McClelland owns: acclaimed Back Bay fine dining spot L'Espalier and the three Sel de la Terre locations—two in Boston and one in a nearby suburb.

"It's kind of a selfish thing I did," admits McClelland. Growing up on his grandparents' farm in New Hampshire gave McClelland early exposure to fresh, seasonal ingredients, and he's been dedicated to working this way throughout his career as a chef and restaurateur. Although running Apple Street means McClelland's days are up to sixteen hours long (he does most of the produce deliveries to the restaurants in the evening), as a lifelong cook and gardener, turning to farming was a natural progression, he says.

L'Espalier is a Boston institution. It's the kind of place where couples get engaged and celebrate their anniversaries, and the kitchen has been a training ground for some of Boston's most talented chefs, such as Barry Maiden of Hungry Mother and Jeremy Sewall of Lineage and Island Creek Oyster Bar. "I've seen thousands of cooks go through the kitchen," says McClelland. "It's the favorite thing of my career—seeing people go through and then elevate themselves."

McClelland bought the restaurant in 1988, when it was located in a townhouse on Gloucester Street in the Back Bay. (It's since moved around the corner to Boylston Street.) From the start, he's defined his style as "haute cuisine New England." He kept a rooftop kitchen garden at the original location, changes his menu daily, and has long supported local growers. "My philosophy has always been, whatever a really good grower produces, we'll use it instantly."

Now he is that grower. After just two years, the farm expanded from three acres to fourteen, added a heated greenhouse, and began raising a small herd of goats. Produce plans are made with his restaurants in mind, and McClelland's chefs can suggest varieties that interest them.

Between the two hundred cooks he employs as the CEO of New France, the company that operates the four restaurants and a catering operation, Au Soleil, "a lot of people are pretty giddy about having the produce come right from the farm," he says. "Cooks often have very little idea what it's like to grow something, so this is exciting for them."

In the restaurants, McClelland's chefs are running Apple Street Dinners, featuring the farm's produce, and McClelland has staged a handful of dinners at Apple Street Farm, where he does all of the cooking. Living on and running the farm has allowed him to get to know the produce in a much more intimate way, he says.

The idea of knowing produce intimately might strike some as frivolous, but for farmers and chefs, it's a critical skill. In this region of

short seasons and constantly changing weather, a week of cold nights can make a big difference in the way a tomato tastes, for example. That's the beauty of farming and cooking for McClelland. Being here on the farm, he says, allows him to understand the cycles of his ingredients in depth.

When he can understand when certain items are perfect, at least one part of his job just got easier. "Cooking is just about highlighting the perfection of that item," McClelland says. Figuring out how to make his small-scale agriculture venture viable? That's the tough part.

Pot-au-Feu of Poussin
with Spring Vegetables and Foie Gras

Serves 6

5 shallots, minced
1/4 c. port
1 c. chicken broth
1 750-ml bottle Pinot Noir
1 bouquet garni (3 stems each of parsley, thyme, and sage,
   tied together with butcher twine)
3 whole black peppercorns
3 Cornish game hens, washed and patted dry, legs trussed
2 leeks, washed and cut into thirds
12 carrots, peeled and cut into chunks
12 turnips, peeled and cut into chunks
12 fingerling potatoes
3 celery stalks, cut into thirds
12 pearl onions
1 tbsp. fresh flat-leaf parsley, minced
1 tbsp. fresh thyme leaves, minced
1 tbsp. fresh sage, minced
salt and freshly ground black pepper

Prepare a bouillon by combining the shallots, port, chicken broth, Pinot Noir, bouquet garni, and peppercorns in a large saucepan over medium heat. Bring to a simmer and cook for 5 minutes, then reduce the heat to low.

Submerge the game hens in the bouillon (it's safer if you do this over low heat). Turn the heat up to medium to bring the liquid back to a simmer, then turn the heat back down to low and cook for 15 minutes. Remove the game hens from the bouillon and set aside. Immediately add the leeks, carrots, turnips, potatoes, celery, and onions to the bouillon. Turn the heat up to medium-low to bring the liquid to a light simmer, then turn the heat back down to low and cook for 10 minutes.

While the vegetables are cooking, remove the game hen meat from the bones and divide it among six bowls. When the vegetables are cooked, remove and discard the bouquet garni, lift the vegetables from the bouillon with a slotted spoon, and distribute them among the bowls. Sprinkle the parsley, thyme, and sage over each portion. Taste the bouillon for seasoning and add salt and pepper if desired. Ladle the bouillon over the contents of each bowl, and serve.

* For a luxurious addition to this pot-au-feu, add 1 lb. Grade A foie gras to the bouillon with all of the vegetables and simmer for 8 minutes. After you've distributed the game hen meat and the vegetables among the six bowls, remove the foie gras from the pot and slice it into six pieces. Add one piece to each bowl, then ladle the bouillon over the contents of each bowl and serve.

Peas

A pea vine trailing on a trellis is one of the most charming plants in a vegetable garden, and home cooks and gardeners also appreciate the sweetness of a just-picked pea, before the sugars have time to convert to starch. But cooks will also tell you that frozen peas are often preferable to fresh because they're flash-frozen and packed before they lose their sweetness. Frozen peas give you bright green color and delicate flavor year-round, so use them liberally. Toss with pasta, rice, or steamed carrots and a pat of butter; turn them into a sauce or even a filling for ravioli. And when it's time to eat peas in season, do it in the garden (or eat them as soon after picking as possible).

Porcini Ravioli
with Pea Pesto

Porcini Ravioli with Pea Pesto

Yield: 30 small ravioli

Consider this a gourmet version of the picnic basket staple pasta salad. Ravioli is always a hit, and the earthy mushrooms and sweet pea flavors in this version make it especially popular.

4 tbsp. butter

4 shallots, finely chopped

2 garlic cloves, minced

3 oz. dried porcini mushrooms, reconstituted (see below) and finely chopped

4 scallions, finely chopped

2 tsp. Worcestershire sauce

1/2 c. freshly grated Parmesan cheese

salt and freshly ground black pepper, to taste

1 recipe Pasta Dough (or 1 lb. store-bought fresh pasta sheets)

2 egg whites, beaten

Melt the butter in a medium-sized saucepan over medium-low heat. Add the shallots and cook until slightly golden, about 6 minutes. Add the garlic and mushrooms and cook on low heat, stirring with a wooden spoon, for 8–10 minutes, or until the mixture has a paste-like consistency. Remove from the heat and add the scallions, Worcestershire sauce, and Parmesan. Season with salt and pepper to taste and set aside to cool.

To make the ravioli: If you're using a pasta machine, roll out the dough on the thinnest setting. If using a rolling pin, dust the countertop with flour, place half the dough on the counter, and continually roll and flip until it is as thin as possible (about 1/16 inch). Form the ravioli by cutting out rounds (or any shape you like) approximately 2 1/2 inches in diameter with a cookie cutter. Press the scraps back together and re-roll the dough. Continue cutting rounds. (You should have sixty total.)

Work with two rounds at a time. Brush them both on one side with the beaten egg white. Place a heaping tablespoon of the mushroom mixture in the center of the egg-washed side of one round and press the other round on top, egg-washed side down. Seal all the edges with your fingers. Set aside on a floured baking sheet while you make the rest of the ravioli. You can make the ravioli ahead to this point and refrigerate them for 1 day or freeze them for up to 1 month.

When all your ravioli are made, fill a medium-sized pot halfway with salted water and bring to a boil over high heat. When the water is boiling, add the ravioli. They are done when they float to the top of the water, which should take about 3 minutes. Gently toss the cooked ravioli with the Pea Pesto (recipe follows) and serve warm or at room temperature.

Cooking with Dried Mushrooms: To reconstitute dried mushrooms, soak them in hot water for 20–30 minutes, then drain before using.

PEA PESTO:

1 c. fresh or frozen peas, blanched

1/2 c. fresh mint leaves

1 tbsp. white onion, finely chopped

1 clove garlic, minced

1/2 c. extra virgin olive oil

2 tbsp. water (or stock, if you have it on hand)

pinch cayenne pepper

salt and freshly ground black pepper, to taste

Combine the peas, mint, onion, garlic, oil, water (or stock), cayenne, salt, and pepper in a blender and purée until you have a pourable consistency. (If it's too thick, add more water, 1 tbsp. at a time, and purée again.)

PASTA DOUGH:

1 c. durum semolina flour

1 c. all-purpose flour

1 tsp. salt

4 large egg yolks

1 large egg

1/2 tsp. olive oil

2 tsp. milk

Combine the flours and salt in the bowl of an electric mixer. Beat the yolks, egg, olive oil, and milk into the dry ingredients until combined. Knead on a lightly floured surface for 3–4 minutes. Wrap tightly in plastic wrap and let rest for 1 hour or up to overnight in the refrigerator before using.

Meritage,
Boston Harbor Hotel

Chef Daniel Bruce
City Growers

"I knew since I could move a chair from the table to the cupboard that I was going to be a chef," says Daniel Bruce, who for twenty-three years has helmed the kitchen at Meritage in the Boston Harbor Hotel.

During his childhood in Cornish, New Hampshire, Bruce says his family was not big into food. "We never went out to eat, ever—I'm not sure where the interest in food came from," he admits. "I can't explain it, really. It's just who I am." As a kid, Bruce cooked for his family to the extent his dad would allow it. Back then, says the chef, "cooking was not looked on as the noble profession it is today."

After attending culinary school at Johnson and Wales in Rhode Island, Bruce moved to Europe for more training. He returned to cook in New York City before heading home to New England, where he landed, for good, at the Boston Harbor Hotel. In his time at the hotel, he has built a strong team—many of his cooks have been with him for more than a dozen years—a deep network of suppliers, and a reputation for Meritage as one of the city's most inventive hotel restaurants.

Although Bruce grew up in New Hampshire, went to high school in Maine and culinary school in Rhode Island, and has been living and working in Massachusetts for more than two decades, he doesn't consider his cuisine New England–focused. "I have a sensibility that's New England–based," he says, but he describes his food as wine-influenced New American.

"Wine-influenced food is my niche, for sure," says Bruce, whose menu at Meritage is organized by wine types—with certain dishes appearing under "light whites" or "robust reds." Bruce also developed the Boston Wine Festival, a three-month series of wine dinners, held at Meritage and hosted by vintners from all over the world.

New England's seasons do influence Bruce's cooking, however—from the varying depth and intensity of his dishes over the course of the year to ingredients featured at their seasonal peak. And with any ingredient he brings into the restaurant, he says, "I try to bring it all the way from the point of origin to the finish." Doing most of the value-added production in house gives him more control over the quality and lets high-quality ingredients stand out.

Many of his best ingredients, especially in the height of the growing season, are sourced from the region. Bruce has been able to develop strong relationships with certain farmers because of the high volume of produce he regularly buys. "They can make one stop and sell 190 pounds of tomatoes," he explains. "I've had great success working that way."

With City Growers, the urban agriculture startup based in Dorchester, Bruce hopes to build a relationship that allows him to define his standards and get what he needs in the volume he needs it—while supporting an important program.

In 2010, social entrepreneur Glynn Lloyd started City Growers to address local food access in urban neighborhoods and train

unemployed urban residents in the agriculture field. "Everyone should have access to local food," he says.

Parts of Dorchester and Roxbury are low-income neighborhoods with high unemployment rates where even grocery stores, let alone farmers' markets or other local food vendors, are hard to come by. One thing these neighborhoods do have is a lot of is vacant land—about 800 acres of it, Lloyd estimates—that can't be redeveloped but is ripe for reclamation.

Lloyd and his team started small in the 2010 growing season, growing greens, tomatoes, basil, and other produce on a 10,000-square-foot plot in Roxbury. A lead grower trains a staff of young apprentices from the neighborhood. Ideally, explains Lloyd, "we're creating jobs and showing that urban agriculture can be a profitable enterprise."

Lloyd's hyper-local approach benefits residents of both the neighborhood and the city as a whole. Lloyd's CSA program accepts food stamps. Adjacent to Roxbury in Jamaica Plain, a number of bakeries and cafés buy produce from City Growers. "Freshness is the value," says Lloyd. "They're getting lettuce picked an hour beforehand."

Targeting higher-end restaurants like Meritage is also part of Lloyd's strategy. As City Growers expands, he hopes to have plots of land dedicated to specific restaurants. "Chefs love the idea," he says. "They get bragging rights to having a plot of land that's customized to what they want." And for the apprentices, producing food for high-profile restaurants is an incentive. "You can't tell me there is someone growing food in Dorchester or Roxbury who isn't excited to deliver food to fancy restaurants."

Yellow Bean, Asparagus, Arugula, and Cherry Tomato Salad

Serves 8

1 c. yellow wax or Romano beans, trimmed
1 lb. asparagus, cut on the bias into 3-inch pieces
1 c. red cherry tomatoes, rinsed, stems removed
1 c. yellow cherry tomatoes, rinsed, stems removed
2 c. baby arugula, washed and dried
2 tbsp. fresh tarragon, chopped
3 tbsp. olive oil
1 tbsp. balsamic vinegar
sea salt and cracked black pepper to taste
1/2 c. Parmesan cheese, grated

Bring a large pot of salted water to a boil. Prepare an ice bath in the sink. When water boils, blanch asparagus until bright green (about 2–3 minutes, depending on the thickness of the stalks). Drain and submerge in the ice bath.

Repeat procedure for beans, allowing time for beans to cook until tender (about 5 minutes). Drain and submerge in the ice bath.

Place asparagus, beans, tomatoes, arugula, and tarragon in a large serving bowl. Toss together. Add olive oil and toss until vegetables are coated. Sprinkle with the vinegar and season with salt and pepper. Garnish with Parmesan cheese and serve.

Strawberry and Buttermilk Shortcakes

Serves 8

BISCUITS:

 1 c. all-purpose flour
 1 tbsp. baking powder
 1 tbsp. sugar
 1/2 stick unsalted butter (4 tbsp.)
 1/2 c. buttermilk
 1/2 tsp. vanilla
 1 large egg

Set the oven to 375 degrees. Place sifted dry ingredients in a bowl and stir together. Cut butter into thin slices and carefully mix by hand into the flour mix. (Do not over mix because this causes biscuits to become tough.) Make a well in the center and add the buttermilk and vanilla. Mix together only until dough is formed. Lay mix onto a floured counter, roll out to 1/2 inch thick, and cut into 3-inch circles. In a small bowl, beat the egg. Place biscuits onto a cookie sheet and brush with the eaten egg. Bake at 375 degrees for approximately 10 minutes or until biscuits are a light brown. Remove from oven and set aside.

STRAWBERRIES:

 4 c. fresh strawberries
 1/2 c. granulated sugar
 1 tsp. vanilla

Rinse and hull strawberries, cut into quarters, and place into a large bowl with sugar and vanilla. Toss together and let sit for at least 1 hour to allow strawberries and sugar to create thick juice.

WHIPPED CREAM:

 1 c. heavy cream
 3 tbs. sugar
 1/2 tsp. vanilla
 powdered sugar for dusting

Place cream, sugar, and vanilla in a bowl and whip until it forms soft peaks.

To assemble shortcakes: Cut biscuits in half. Place the bottom halves on plates. Top with 1/2 c. strawberries and a dollop of whipped cream. Place the tops of the biscuits on the cream and finish with a dusting of powdered sugar.

Strawberries

There's a bit of a frenzy surrounding strawberries every June when they first hit the market. They're the first fruit of the season, and their window of availability is narrow—three or four weeks, tops. Fragile native berries are a world apart from the standard supermarket varieties, which are shipped from California and can't rival the natives for fragrance, juiciness, and rich, clear flavor. Members of the rose family, wild strawberries grew in both the New and Old Worlds before being cultivated first in Europe and later in the American colonies. When shopping for berries at the farmers' market, look for firm, fragrant fruits with their green caps still attached. Rinse only right before using, and store in the fridge—if they don't disappear in a feeding frenzy first.

Ten Tables

Proprietor Krista Kranyak
Allandale Farm

With her daughter's third Ten Tables restaurant now humming in Provincetown on Cape Cod, Krista Kranyak's mother must be relieved.

In 1999, Kranyak moved to San Francisco for graduate school. Despite having worked in restaurants since she was fifteen, she was planning to become a therapist. When she arrived, she says, "I realized I didn't want to be in grad school. My mother freaked out." She came back to Boston a month later to get serious about restaurant work, and, she continues, "I promised my mother I'd own my own place by the time I was thirty."

The first location opened in Jamaica Plain more than ten years ago, the day after her thirtieth birthday. It's now a neighborhood institution, with a packed house almost every night of the week. According to Kranyak, the restaurant endures, in part, because of its affordable menu and consistently good food. The other part has been the service style cultivated by Kranyak and her staff. "Hospitality has always been second nature to me," she says. "I learned that from my mom. Be kind, and listen to what people want. It's not hard to make them have a good time." As a result, nightly service feels like a dinner party at her place. "We have a lot of regulars, a lot of standing reservations. We're just part of the neighborhood."

Running the neighborhood bistro has long been Kranyak's intent. When she was planning Ten Tables, she traveled to France and Italy, eating and "checking out different places until I got a sense of what I wanted—the owner waiting tables, that kind of thing."

Serving locally grown food is part of the concept. Kranyak has worked with farms like Verrill in Concord and Allandale in Brookline since the get-go, and puts together farmers' market menus from shopping trips during the growing season. Because the restaurants and menus are small, Kranyak and her staff can build close relationships with farms and change menus regularly. She works closely with her chefs, who tweak the menus daily to keep the European-inspired food tuned to New England's seasons. "This is the kind of food everyone should have on their table," says Kranyak. Close proximity and a good relationship with local farmers helps Kranyak get the best food on her tables, although now with three locations, she has many more than ten.

One of Kranyak's favorite farms is Allandale, near her Jamaica Plain location in Brookline. On a snowy day in January, Allandale Farm's head grower Jim Buckle is getting ready to fly to Puerto Rico for a short vacation. You'd think this urban farm just outside Boston would be slow enough in the winter to enable the farmers to escape for longer than a week, but this is a busy, growing enterprise. There are seed orders to place, crop plans to hash out, CSA members to sign up, and a summer education program to organize.

It pays to be organized, literally, says farm manager John Lee, who has run Allandale's farm operations for more than twenty-five years. "In the Northeast you get six months to make all your money,"

he says. So from bedding plants to heirloom produce to Christmas trees, the more ways the farm can engage its customers, the better.

When Lee first came to Allandale in the mid-1980s, it was a small business selling corn on the honor system, run by two brothers who realized they'd need to bring in a full-time farmer in order to keep the land in agriculture. (Allandale is in a high-income residential neighborhood and down the street from a hospital.) They hired Lee, who in the beginning was "farmer, bookkeeper, mechanic, store manager, etcetera," he says. He's since built the farm into a Boston institution with a farm crew of fourteen and a 430-person CSA.

Allandale's produce is featured mostly on menus in Boston where head grower Buckle is friendly with the restaurant owners and chefs. "The restaurants are not a big focus for us," he says, "so I like to know the people and feel comfortable communicating with them."

Still, many chefs come to the farm store as retail customers or to pick up wholesale orders. The lure of this serene but bustling farm in the middle of the city is a draw for people, and that's the way Lee and Buckle like it. "It's important for us to be largely retail," says Lee. "People need to know where their food is coming from and how it's being produced. We need people to feel ownership."

Rhubarb Upside-Down Cake

Serves 6–8

1 c. sugar
1/4 c. water
1/4 c. unsalted butter, cut into small chunks
3 medium stalks rhubarb, trimmed, peeled (if tough), and
   chopped into 1/2-inch pieces
1 1/2 c. all-purpose flour
2 tsp. baking powder
1/2 tsp. salt
1/2 c. unsalted butter, melted and cooled
1 c. sugar
2 large eggs, at room temperature
1/2 c. buttermilk
1 tbsp. vanilla extract

Grease a 10-inch cake pan with butter and set aside. Set the oven to 350 degrees.

Make the caramel: In a 2-quart saucepan, combine the sugar and water and cook over medium heat, stirring constantly until the sugar is a light amber color. Watch the sugar carefully to make sure it doesn't burn. Remove from the heat and whisk in the butter a couple of pieces at a time. Pour the caramel into the cake pan and scatter the rhubarb in an even layer over the caramel. Set aside.

Make the batter: In a small bowl, whisk together the flour, baking powder, and salt.

In a standing mixer or a large mixing bowl with a hand mixer, whisk together the melted butter and sugar until light and foamy. Add the eggs one at a time and beat until thoroughly combined. Add the buttermilk and vanilla and mix until the batter is light and fluffy. Add a third of the flour mixture and mix to combine. Repeat twice until all of the flour is incorporated. Pour the batter over the rhubarb and caramel and smooth over the top.

Place the cake pan on a baking sheet and bake for about 50 minutes, rotating halfway through. The cake should be golden and shrinking away from the sides of the pan. Place the cake pan onto a cooling rack and let cool for 10–15 minutes. Then invert onto a plate or platter to cool completely.

Asparagus Soup

Serves 6–8

1/2 stick unsalted butter (4 tbsp.)
1 small onion, chopped into 1-inch pieces
1 leek, cleaned, trimmed, and chopped into 1-inch pieces
1 garlic clove, chopped
1 yellow potato, peeled and chopped into 1-inch pieces
1 1/2 lbs. asparagus, trimmed and cut into 2-inch pieces
4 c. vegetable stock
2 c. baby spinach leaves, rinsed
1 c. heavy cream
salt and pepper to taste (preferably white pepper)

Place a Dutch oven or a soup pot over medium heat. Add the butter, and when it foams, add the onion and leeks. Cook, stirring occasionally, until the onions and leeks have softened and turned partially translucent but not browned. Add the garlic and cook for a minute or two more to soften it. Add the potato and asparagus; stir to combine with the onion mixture. Cook for 5 minutes over medium heat until the asparagus begins to soften.

Increase heat to high, add the vegetable stock, and bring to a boil. Reduce heat to medium-low and simmer until asparagus is tender (about 10 minutes). Add the spinach leaves and cook until they've wilted into the soup.

Purée using an immersion blender or transfer soup in small batches to a blender and process until smooth. If desired, pass purée through a strainer. Return the puréed soup to the pot. With the heat on low, add the cream and heat through. Season to taste with salt and pepper and serve.

Rhubarb

Rhubarb, also known as "pieplant," can be baffling for some cooks, especially the baking-averse. The tart, astringent vegetable is used as a fruit and known best as a natural partner to strawberries. They're ready at the same time of year, and rhubarb's tartness, from oxalic acid, sets off the berries' sweetness. Rhubarb is most often used in pies, crumbles, and jams. But it also sparkles when processed into a syrup for cordials, baked with honey and served over yogurt or ice cream, or served over lamb or pork as an ingredient in a savory compote. Rhubarb stalks range in color from pale green and pink to deep red and should be firm and unblemished when purchased.

summer

No matter how tough the winter seems, it fades into memory as soon as the first days of summer arrive. The beaches fill up with bright umbrellas and little kids building sandcastles. Long days in the sun hit their perfect end with a bottle of beer, a bag of corn for shucking, and a pot of water for the lobsters. Dinners can be that simple, or they can be more composed, using some of the recipes featured here. Whichever direction you head, in the summertime, good eating is easy.

Hamersley's Bistro

Chef Gordon Hamersley
Blue Heron Farm

With his restaurant—and his Red Sox hat—a fixture in Boston's South End, Gordon Hamersley is known for his regional French-inspired food, anchored by New England ingredients.

When he opened Hamersley's Bistro in 1987, he says, "I was one of the first people to latch on to the idea that local food does a couple of important things: It provides fun and entertainment for the chefs and farmers—we get to know each other. Diners get a better sense of where their food is coming from. And, it's cheaper and tastes better."

Twenty-five years later, says the chef, "I don't even talk about local farms and farmers that much on my menu. People who know me know that it's not a marketing scheme for me, it's just what I do."

Hamersley got his start in the restaurant business in spite of himself, he insists. After college, the job market wasn't clicking. "I needed a job," he says. "I'd never had a passion for cooking—I had a passion for eating. And working in a restaurant was a good way to get a meal every day." He found work as a dishwasher in a French bistro in Cambridge, where he was introduced to a whole new world of restaurants and cooking. "I started learning about why certain dishes get cooked in certain areas of the world, and it opened up a curiosity in me that has never waned."

Hamersley started cooking at a time when New American cuisine was taking shape. Hooked on the business, Hamersley moved to California and found work with Wolfgang Puck, whose game-changing food, says Hamersley, "opened up my eyes to what the potential of food could be."

From California, Hamersley traveled to France, where the inspiration for his own bistro began percolating. He and his wife, Fiona, traversed the country, eating in bistros everywhere. "Wherever we went," he says, "we noticed that things changed—the food, the mood, the feeling—depending on the region: Alsace, Normandy, Brittany, southwestern France, Provence. We decided when we came back to Boston, we'd open a French bistro and say that New England is our region."

Although Hamersley's is inspired by French regional cooking, the food is shaped by New England's seasons and ingredients. "I always say we have six seasons in New England," comments Hamersley. "Look at the difference between September and November." Although he doesn't interpret Yankee cooking per se, Hamersley says his food can't help but be influenced by New England culinary traditions because the traditions are bound to the place. "The growing season in New England is incredibly short," he points out. "So our history is all about preserving—canning, freezing, drying, and so on. Getting through the winter: that's what we do."

And after twenty years of cooking in Boston, Hamersley sees more and more cooks working locally and seasonally and practicing the techniques that tie their food to New England. "The common denominator is local waters, local farms, ranchers, artisans," explains

Hamersley. "That's what roots us all together. The sea, the seasons—we celebrate the things that make sense to us."

Speaking of roots, Ellery Kimball of Blue Heron Farm has been farming the same piece of land for eighteen years, since the day she started as a summer intern following her senior year of high school. "After the first day working there I pretty much knew I wanted to be a farmer," she says. Feeling that sense of certainty about her career path, says Kimball, is "pretty much akin to finding the man of your dreams."

The seven-acre Blue Heron Farm in Lincoln, Massachusetts—about thirty minutes outside Boston—is located on town conservation land. Kimball grew up practically next door. After studying sustainable agriculture in college and working summers on the farm, she continued working there after graduation until her boss was ready to move on. Then, she inherited the lease. Kimball has been running the farm since 2001.

In addition to the farm stand and two farmers' markets that Blue Heron goes to, Kimball also sells her organic produce to about a dozen restaurants, which accounts for about 50 percent of her sales. "It's wonderful to sell to people who really know how to cook your food," she says.

Kimball believes her relationships with her restaurant customers have also made her a better farmer, cook, and salesperson. "Working with chefs allows me to grow different things that I wouldn't necessarily be able to sell at the farm stand," she says. "It gets me excited about cooking too, and makes it easier for me to sell the vegetables. Chefs have also taught me a lot about the things I grow—when to harvest them for the best flavor and so on," continues Kimball.

And Kimball limits the chefs she works with to those she connects with personally and who share her passion for seasonal and organic produce. "It's kind of like dating," she says. "When I seek out a chef, it doesn't really last sometimes—but when a chef seeks me out, it means they are invested and want to make it work."

Charred Mackerel with Minty Red Currant Caponata and Toasted Pine Nuts

Serves 4

Mackerel fillets can weigh as little as 1 1/2 to 2 oz. and as much as 5 to 6. Try to choose medium-sized fillets and cut them to size so that each person gets two pieces of about 3 oz. each.

1/4 c. olive oil

1/2 medium onion, peeled and minced (about 1 c.)

2 stalks celery, peeled and cut into a 1/4-inch dice (about 1 c.)

3 tbsp. red currants

1 pinch red pepper flakes

1/2 eggplant, peeled and cut into a 1/4-inch dice (about 4 c.)

1 tsp. salt

1 tsp. sugar

3 tsp. red wine vinegar

1/2 c. tomato juice

10–12 leaves fresh mint, chopped

1 medium scallion, cut into thin rounds

2 tbsp. cooking oil

fillets of super fresh mackerel, pin bones removed (about 6 oz. per person)

3 tbsp. pine nuts, toasted and crushed

lemon slices

mint leaves

In a large sauté pan, heat the olive oil until it is hot but not smoking. Add the onion and celery and cook for 3–4 minutes, stirring frequently. Add the red currants and red pepper flakes and stir to combine. Add the eggplant and continue to cook, stirring, for an additional 6–8 minutes. The eggplant will have absorbed the moisture in the pan and begun to cook down at this point. Add the salt and sugar and cook an additional 2–3 minutes. Add the red wine vinegar and tomato juice. Continue to cook over moderate heat for about 6–8 more minutes. The liquids will have been absorbed into the eggplant mixture. Transfer to a bowl and set aside to cool.

When the eggplant mixture has cooled to room temperature, add the chopped mint and scallion rounds and more salt if needed. Stir to combine. Reserve. *Note: This can be done up to two days in advance and kept cold in the refrigerator. When ready to use, let the caponata come to room temperature.*

In a large sauté pan large enough to hold the mackerel fillets without them touching, heat 2 tbsp. cooking oil. It is good to use more than one pan to do this so you have plenty of room. Sprinkle the fish with salt and black pepper. When the oil is very hot, almost smoking, add the fish, skin side down, and let brown for about 3 minutes. Do not shake the pan or move the fish as it cooks! As the fish begins to turn whitish grey around the edges you know that the skin is charred and crispy.

Carefully turn each fish fillet over and then turn off the heat. Allow the fish to finish cooking in the pan (about 3 minutes depending on the size of the fish).

To serve: Divide the caponata among four plates. Squeeze lemon juice over the mackerel fillets and then transfer them to sit on top of the caponata. Sprinkle the toasted pine nuts on the top and drizzle a few more drops of olive oil around the plate. Finally, sprinkle some mint leaves around the plates and serve with lemon slices.

Summer Squash

To the Narragansett Indians, squash meant "a green thing, eaten raw," according to food expert Harold McGee. Today, squash—namely, summer squash—means the big green vegetable offered by a gardening neighbor whose plot is overrun by the vigorous plants. Prolific in the garden, summer squash is also versatile in the kitchen. As Native Americans attested, it can be eaten raw—best shredded and tossed with vinaigrette or quickly pickled— or it can be added to baked goods, fried, sautéed, stuffed, or broiled. A member of the cucurbit family that includes the thick-skinned winter squashes like acorn and butternut, summer squash varieties include zucchini, pattypan, and crookneck.

Gratin of Zucchini
with Jacob's Cattle Beans and Basil

Serves 4–6

4 tbsp. olive oil or cooking oil

1/2 white onion, peeled and diced

1/2 c. dried Jacob's cattle beans, soaked for 6–8 hours or overnight *(Note: A canned cooked bean will work for this recipe. Try cannellini or lima.)*

1 medium zucchini, cut into 3 slices about 7 inches long by about 1/4 inch thick

3 cloves garlic, peeled and sliced very thin

3/4 c. heavy cream

8–10 leaves basil, washed and torn into pieces (do this at the last second for best flavor)

1 tbsp. lemon juice

1/2 c. Asiago cheese, grated

salt and pepper to taste

1/2 c. coarse breadcrumbs, toasted until golden brown

Heat 2 tbsp. oil in a large saucepan and add the onion. Cook for 3–4 minutes until it is translucent. Drain the beans; add them to the pot with water to cover the beans by about 2–3 inches. Bring to a boil and then lower the heat to a simmer. Cook the beans until they are very soft and tender (about 2 1/2–3 hours, depending on the soaking time and how old they are).

Drain and reserve. This should yield about 2 c. cooked beans and onion mixture. This can be done well in advance or the day before. Store in the refrigerator.

Set the oven to 375 degrees. Heat the remaining olive oil in a sauté pan over medium heat until hot but not smoking. Sprinkle the zucchini with salt and pepper and place slices cut side down in the pan. Cook over medium heat until the zucchini is nicely golden brown on one side. Turn the zucchini over, lower the heat, and continue to cook until they are tender (about 6–8 minutes total cooking time). Add the garlic slices and continue to cook for 1 minute. The zucchini should be tender when pierced with the tip of a knife. Set aside.

In a small saucepan, bring the cream to a boil.

In a large mixing bowl, place 2 c. of the cooked beans, basil, lemon juice, 1/4 c. Asiago cheese, and salt and pepper to taste. Toss to combine. Pour the hot cream over the bean mixture and stir well to combine.

Spread the bean mixture evenly into a 1 1/2-qt. gratin dish. Lay the browned zucchini slices and garlic on top of the beans in an even layer so that the surface of the beans is more or less covered with the zucchini slices. Sprinkle with the remaining cheese and then the toasted breadcrumbs.

Place the gratin dish in the oven and bake for about 15–20 minutes or until the zucchini is quite tender and hot, the breadcrumbs are brown and crispy, and the creamy mixture is bubbling. Allow to rest for 10–15 minutes before serving.

Oleana

Chef Ana Sortun
Siena Farms

Ingredients are important to Ana Sortun. Growing up in Seattle in a food-savvy family, she was raised on homemade butter and fresh fish. She studied cooking in France, where shopping at the farmers' market was part of the curriculum. Today, Sortun is extra-close to the source of her ingredients—her husband Chris Kurth's Siena Farms supplies Sortun's acclaimed restaurant Oleana with the bulk of its produce throughout the year.

Sortun's parents had grown up on farms, she says, and as a kid, "my parents and grandparents were sticklers for good ingredients. We weren't allowed to eat junk food. My mother, grandmother, and great-grandmother were all really good cooks. And we always had simple meals with really good ingredients. Those things you learn never really go away." Sortun, who started working in restaurants at age fourteen, started cooking when she was sixteen and enrolled in culinary school at age nineteen.

Although Sortun has spent the better part of her career in Boston, and most of her ingredients are grown twenty-five miles west of Boston, her food is inspired by another part of the world. When she arrived in Boston in the early 1990s, she helped an early player on the Boston restaurant scene, Moncef Meddeb, open Aigo Bistro. Meddeb's food was Mediterranean-inspired, and Sortun took to it, working under the chef for years.

She continued cooking food from the Spanish and French Mediterranean at restaurants after Aigo until a trip to Turkey shifted her interests. "I was completely blown away," she says, "by the flavors, the use of spices, the styles of eating, the way meals were composed—everything."

"I made a study of the food," says Sortun, who returns to Turkey regularly. "It's something my heart really relates to." Oleana opened in 2001, introducing area diners to spices like za'atar and sumac and dishes like quail with baharat and barberries or tuna kibbeh nayeh. For more than a decade, dinner at Oleana has remained one of the most delightful dining experiences in town.

Part of that charm comes from the restaurant's warm, personal character, which Siena Farms helps to define. "We write our menus around the farm," and living on the farm, says Sortun, has given her insight as a chef that she wouldn't have otherwise encountered.

"It's the nuances of things," she says. "Like, the arugula gets better in the fall, it gets a little spicier then, same with carrots. Or the stages that garlic goes through—flowers, scapes—it blows my mind."

"What it takes to grow and work on the farm—I might not have known that," she continues. "A lot of things I'm privy to have changed me."

Sortun and Kurth met in 2002 when he was working as a farm instructor at the Farm School in Athol, looking to sell produce to Oleana. They married soon after, and in 2005, their daughter Siena was born. By 2006, Siena Farms was up and running in the fields Kurth had grown up on in Sudbury. The fifty-acre farm grows organic produce for a CSA and farmers' markets, and Siena also sells wholesale to many Boston-area restaurants.

Sortun's spice-based, Eastern Mediterranean food is a conversation between the cuisine she's interpreting and the ingredients that bring it to life. It's the Mediterranean by way of Sudbury and Cambridge, Massachusetts.

Heirloom Tomato Kibbeh
with Heirloom Tomato Labne-Stuffed Dolma

Serves 6

2 c. grated tomato with pulp and seeds (2 large heirlooms)

1 green bell pepper, finely minced

1 bunch scallions, finely minced

1 tbsp. red pepper paste (or 1 tsp. harissa)

1 tbsp. tomato paste

2 tsp. ground cumin

3/4 tsp. Aleppo chilies or sweet paprika

1 1/2 c. fine bulgur

salt and pepper

1/2 c. plus 1 tbsp. extra virgin olive oil

6 small Brandywine or yellow heirloom tomatoes

1 1/2 c. labne (strained yogurt)

1 lemon, cut into 6 big wedges to squeeze

Place the grated tomato, minced green pepper, scallions, pepper paste, tomato paste, cumin, and chilies in a bowl. Whisk together and season well with salt and pepper. Stir in fine bulgur and 1/2 c. olive oil. Let sit for 15–20 minutes, stirring from time to time. Fill a medium-sized mixing bowl with ice water.

In a medium-sized saucepan, bring the water to a boil on high heat. Make an *X* with a small paring knife in each of the six yellow or small Brandywine tomatoes. Drop them in the boiling water for 20 seconds or until you see the skin peel back from the tomato. Using a slotted spoon or sieve, remove the tomatoes from the water and plunge them into the bowl of ice water. Remove the skins. Cut each tomato in half lengthwise and remove seeds. Salt each tomato lightly and allow to sit for a few minutes, cut side down, to drain some of the water. Select six beautiful halves for stuffing and finely mince the other six halves for concasse. Chop the minced tomatoes until they start to form a paste. Place them over a sieve and let them drain for 10 minutes to lose some of their water. Place the tomato concasse in a small mixing bowl and season with salt and pepper. Stir in 1 tbsp. olive oil and set aside.

In a small bowl, season the labne with salt and pepper. Stuff each reserved tomato half with 3–4 tbsp. labne. *To serve:* Spread the kibbeh in a round shape on each plate; top with a couple of table-spoons of tomato concasse, some lightly dressed greens, and the stuffed tomato half. Serve with lemon.

Peaches and Nectarines

Members of the same species, *prunus persica* (within the rose family), peaches and nectarines are stone fruits whose season in New England is short-lived but much anticipated. Peaches and nectarines don't store starch in their flesh, which means that they don't ripen as well once picked. So native peaches and nectarines, which aren't shipped long distances, are allowed to ripen and develop sweetness on the tree—making them more flavorful (and more perishable) by the time they get home.

Vermont Quail with Nectarines, Leeks, and Green Harissa

Serves 4 small plates

4 Vermont quail

salt and pepper to taste

2 tsp. Baharat Spice Mix (see recipe below)

4 small leeks (or 2 large)

6 tbsp. olive oil (approximately)

2 tbsp. dry white wine

1 loaf pita bread

2 ripe nectarines

1 tbsp. fresh lemon juice

1 c. Zhoug (see recipe below)

Debone the quail, leaving each half intact by removing the breast off of one side of the carcass and detaching the leg with the bone still left in. Do the same to the other side of the quail so that you have two halves with a boneless breast and a bone-in thigh still attached to each other. Place each half with the skin side down and remove the thigh and leg bone by making an incision near the bone and trimming around it until it cuts right out. Sprinkle each half quail with salt and about 1/4 tsp. Baharat Spice for each half quail (1 tsp. total). Fold the breast over the leg with the skin side on the outside and set aside.

Set the oven to 375 degrees. Remove the dark green part of the leek and cut the white part into 2-inch pieces. Split each piece in half and wash, leaving the leeks intact. Place in a baking dish and season with salt. Add 1 tbsp. olive oil and the wine, and sprinkle with salt and pepper. Cover twice with foil. Place in the oven and braise until soft, about 20–25 minutes. (You can also do this on the stovetop in a pan covered with a lid on low heat with the addition of 2 tbsp. water.)

Split the pita bread in half so that you open the pocket and have two thin sheets of pita. Brush each side generously with olive oil and place on a baking sheet. Toast in the oven until golden brown and crispy (about 8–12 minutes). Cool.

Cut the nectarines into 1/2-inch-thick wedges and place in a small mixing bowl. Combine with 1 tbsp. olive oil and 1 tsp. Baharat. Season with salt to taste. Place on a baking tray and roast in the oven until just tender (about 5–8 minutes, depending on how ripe the fruit is). Drizzle with lemon juice.

Crush the pita in a food processor fitted with a steel blade until you have a fine crumb. Season with salt to taste.

Heat 1 tbsp. olive oil in a sauté pan over medium heat until it is hot and shimmering. Add the quail to the pan and place a weight on top (you can use a panini press or a smaller heavy skillet weighed down further with a can of food). Cook on one side to press the leg meat into the breast meat and crisp the skin (about 3 minutes). Flip and repeat on the other side. Remove from the pan immediately and allow the quail to rest for about 5 minutes.

Spoon the leeks on a plate and top with some of the nectarine slices. Sprinkle generously with pita crumb (about a tablespoon). Top with two pieces of quail and serve with Zhoug on the side.

BAHARAT SPICE MIX:

2 tsp. dried oregano

1 tsp. ground cinnamon

1 tsp. ground nutmeg

1 tsp. ground cumin

1 tsp. ground coriander

2 tsp. dried mint, crushed through a sieve

2 tsp. ground black pepper

1/2 tsp. ground allspice

Mix to combine. Store in an airtight container out of the light for up to 6 months.

ZHOUG (SYRIAN CHILE PASTE):

2 Hungarian wax peppers, roughly chopped

1/2 bunch cilantro, cleaned with a little stem left and roughly chopped

1/2 bunch parsley, cleaned with a little stem left and roughly chopped

1 tsp. garlic, roughly chopped

salt to taste

1/2 tsp. ground coriander

1/2 tsp. ground cumin

1 tsp. white wine vinegar

1/4 c. olive oil

Combine all ingredients except the olive oil in a blender or food processor. With the blender or food processor running, add the oil in a slow stream. You will have a bright green emulsified substance.

Vermont Quail
with Nectarines, Leeks, and Green Harissa

Russell House Tavern

Chef Michael Scelfo
Fiore di Nonno

"I took a long, bumpy journeyman's road that I feel like I'm still on," says Michael Scelfo, assessing his career path. Even while helming the kitchen at high-volume hotspot Russell House Tavern, the self-taught chef says, "I still feel the need to prove myself."

Russell House Tavern, a 240-seat gastro-pub in the center of Harvard Square, opened in April 2010 with Scelfo as executive chef. It's not his first executive position, but it's his most high-profile. Scelfo, whose career began in Portland, Oregon, had big ambitions early on. He never had a sous-chef position before working as an executive chef.

"I had a belief in my abilities," explains Scelfo, who says he talked his way into most of his first jobs. "I felt like I had a creative side that I really wanted to listen to."

Scelfo grew up on Long Island, in a big family that liked to cook and eat together. "I was always into food as a kid," he says. Moving with his family to both Kansas City and California exposed him to different regional cooking styles, although his own heritage of family-style Italian cooking was embedded from an early age.

After enrolling in cooking school in Portland, Scelfo cooked for Cory Schrieber, an early advocate of local and seasonal cooking, at his restaurant, Wildwood. "It was kind of the heyday for cooking in Portland," Scelfo says. It was also his first introduction to working with independent vendors—the mushroom foragers and berry farmers whose ingredients were helping to define Northwest cuisine.

After six years, Scelfo came back east to be closer to his family. A random meeting turned into an offer to be the opening chef at a Boston-area restaurant, Arlington's Tea Tray in the Sky. Scelfo moved in 2001 and has worked in Boston ever since, where, he says, he's had to learn as he goes along.

His style of food, he says, mirrors his career path and has become much more stripped down as Scelfo has matured as a cook. "When I was really young," he says, "I wanted to do too much on the plate. My style has evolved—it's become a de-evolution. I've taken away more than I've added." Although New England is reflected in the ingredients he uses, Scelfo doesn't see himself as cooking New England cuisine. "It's more like modern twists on classic American," he insists.

Cooking this way, says Scelfo, "has to start with good ingredients," something he preaches to his cooks nonstop. "It really begins when you see something for the first time and you realize that this pastured chicken is infinitely better looking and tasting than one that came from a big-box purveyor."

For Scelfo, tracking down the right ingredients has become a central focus. Even in a spot with as moderate a price point and as high a volume of business as Russell House, he says, it's possible to work with local and sustainable food. It means taking on extra legwork in an already jam-packed day, but it's worth the effort. "You just don't entertain the possibility that it's not an option," he continues.

One recent addition to Scelfo's network of suppliers is Lourdes Smith. She is the woman responsible for the burrata. It's hard to stop eating the little purses of fresh mozzarella with a creamy gush of mascarpone in the center—even when faced with Smith's other products, such as the balls of mozzarella or braided string cheese she makes fresh daily at her shop in Somerville.

After spending many years in the restaurant business, she started her own business, Fiore di Nonno, in 2006 as a tribute to her grandfather, an Italian immigrant who owned a dairy shop in Hoboken, New Jersey. As a kid, she says, Smith was fascinated by the mozzarella-making process and the taste of the handmade, still-warm cheese. She apprenticed with the store's current owner in Hoboken and returned to Massachusetts to start building her company.

Even though the company has had 40 percent growth every year since its founding, the business end of things is challenging for Smith. "Making the cheese is one thing," she says. "Running a business is another thing. It's hard for me to sell my cheese."

Actually, the cheese sells itself. It's been featured on prominent restaurant menus all over town since Smith started knocking on restaurant doors five years ago, and the chefs have helped to champion Smith and her products—her cheese has traveled to the James Beard Awards with some of Boston's top chefs. That kind of encouragement and support, says Smith, has helped build "credibility and credence for the product."

Smith also depends on retail and farmers' markets, markets being places where she can interact with customers, get direct feedback about the product, and give cheese-making demonstrations. It's all part of building a loyal customer base, says Smith. Really, all you need to do is taste her burrata, and loyalty will be a given.

Lourdes's Burrata with Olive Oil and Golden Raisin Condiment

Serves 2

2 mascarpone-filled burratini

3 tbsp. golden raisins, soaked in hot tap water for 10 minutes

3 tbsp. walnuts, chopped

1 tbsp. parsley, finely chopped

1 tbsp. chives, sliced very thin

1/2 tsp. red pepper flakes

3 tbsp. extra virgin olive oil

3 slices crusty bread, toasted

salt and pepper

Set the oven to 350 degrees and then bring the cheese to room temperature on the counter (around 25 minutes should do). Place walnuts on a sheet pan and toast until golden brown (around 5–7 minutes). Brush some olive oil on your bread slices and season with salt and pepper; toast until golden (7–9 minutes). Set aside.

Transfer cooled nuts to a medium-sized mixing bowl. Drain the raisins and chop them roughly, then add to the bowl with the walnuts. Add the parsley, chives, pepper flakes, and olive oil and toss gently with a spoon. Season with salt and pepper. Gently halve the cheese and add it to the bowl, rolling it gently in the mix.

Arrange your bread on a plate and carefully transfer the cheese atop the bread. Spoon remaining condiment over the cheese. Sprinkle some good coarse salt and a few whole parsley leaves across the top and serve immediately.

Striped Bass

Arriving in May, the presence of big, beautiful striped bass in rivers and estuaries signifies the coming of summer for many New England anglers—and eaters. A migratory species that's the state fish of Maryland, striped bass are one of the most popular fish among recreational fishermen along the East Coast. For good reason—the schooling fish tend to stay close to shore and cluster around beaches, bays, and estuaries, making them easy to find. They put up a good fight on the fishing line and are generally large—the better for bragging rights. But their flavor and texture is the real prize. The dense, meaty flesh tastes sweet, clean, and briny, like seawater. It pairs well with practically anything but has a special affinity for robust summery flavors like eggplant caponata or fresh or roasted tomatoes.

Pan-Roasted Striped Bass
with Cherry Tomato Vinaigrette
and Mustardy Zucchini

Serves 2

- 2 zucchini, split in half lengthwise
- 1 tbsp. fresh tarragon, chopped
- 2 tsp. Dijon mustard
- 1 1/2 c. ripe cherry tomatoes, quartered
- 1/2 c. plus 3 tbsp. extra virgin olive oil
- 1 tbsp. whole grain mustard
- 1 tbsp. honey
- 1 tbsp. chives, thinly sliced
- 1 tbsp. Italian parsley, roughly chopped
- 1 tbsp. basil, roughly chopped
- 1/4 c. sherry vinegar
- 2 8-oz. pieces wild striped bass, skin on
- salt and pepper

For the zucchini: Whisk together the tarragon, Dijon mustard, and 1 tbsp. olive oil. Season to taste with salt and pepper. Rub mix on zucchini and set aside.

Place the cherry tomatoes in a medium-sized mixing bowl. To make the vinaigrette, whisk together mustard, honey, herbs, and vinegar in a small bowl until combined. Slowly drizzle in 1/2 c. olive oil while whisking vigorously. Pour mix over tomatoes, season to taste, and set aside.

Set the oven to 450 degrees and place a metal baking sheet in the oven while heating.

For the fish: Heat an oven-proof sauté pan with remaining 2 tbsp. olive oil on high until oil is shimmering hot. Season the fish fillets with salt and pepper and gently place the fish in the pan, skin side down. Do not shake the pan or move the fish. Watch the fish until it begins to appear golden brown around the skin, then transfer the pan into the oven and let the fish continue to cook, skin side down for an additional 7–9 minutes.

When you place the fish in the oven, place the zucchini cut side down on the hot baking sheet that's been heating in the oven.

Remove the fish and the zucchini from the oven at the same time. Fish should seem fairly firm to the touch. Remove from the pan and allow to rest on a cutting board or platter for a few minutes before serving. Arrange the zucchini on a plate and place fish skin side up to be served. Take some tomatoes from the vinaigrette and arrange on top of the bass. Drizzle some of the vinaigrette as you see fit.

Clover Food Lab

Rolando Rebledo
Farm Fresh Rhode Island's Market Mobile

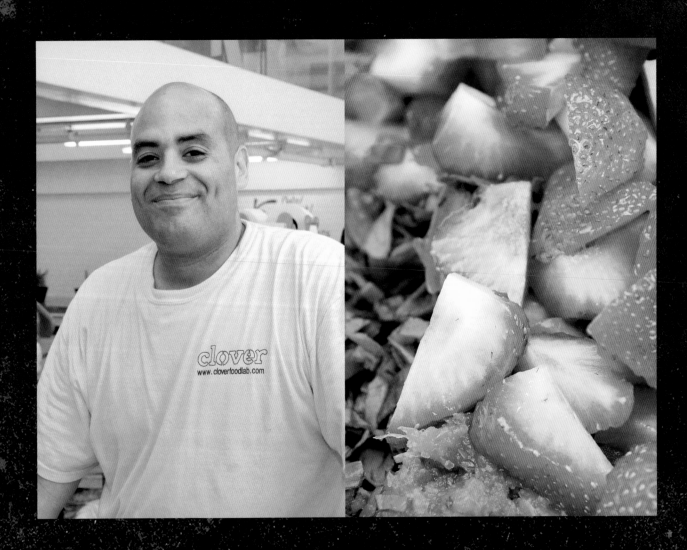

Tucked down a side street in suburban Winchester Center, Parsons Table is a cozy neighborhood spot that feels as if it has been there for years. Because it has—sort of. Chris and Megan Parsons have been running a restaurant here since opening Catch in 2003, but in 2010 they switched up the restaurant's concept, menu, and name.

Well-loved Catch had developed into more of a fine dining restaurant than Chris Parsons had anticipated, and while they wanted to expand, they also didn't want to lose their space in Winchester. "It feels very natural doing business here," says Chris. "The customers I don't really consider customers anymore. They're friends."

So without abandoning his friends, Parsons gave them something new: a relaxed restaurant with an approachable, affordable menu that doesn't take any shortcuts. "We put the same amount of effort and care into each dish," says Parsons. "Our core values—treating ingredients with respect, quality local ingredients executed properly—that hasn't changed."

In seven years as the chef/owner of Catch, Parsons built the restaurant's reputation as one of the best seafood restaurants in the Boston area. His affinity for fish, he says, comes from growing up fly-fishing with his father and spending summers in East Dennis on Cape Cod, fishing for bluefish and striped bass.

Growing up eating fresh local seafood gave Parsons an understanding of what he wanted to accomplish in his own restaurant. After graduating from Johnson and Wales and doing a stint cooking in Colorado, Parsons returned to the Boston area and worked as a chef in a number of restaurants (including as the opening chef for his friend Joanne Chang's Flour Bakery and Café) before opening his own.

As a chef, "the goal is to get great product," says Parsons. With seafood, that means building his network of suppliers to include as many direct relationships as possible. "We're always trying to grow and expand our network."

In the Boston area, working directly with fishermen is not common, but it's possible. In the past few years, as wholesale prices have dropped and fishing regulations have become more restrictive, some fishermen have taken advantage of the interest in local foods and set up shop at the farmers' markets or approached chefs directly.

According to Parsons, in the conventional seafood business, information about the fish is easily obscured. "When you get it right from the source, it's easy to know if it's fresh and where it came from," he says. And customers respond to knowing where the fish is from. "I think it comes from people knowing and caring more about the environment—people don't want to be eating things that aren't good for the world around them."

At Parsons Table, friends and customers won't have to worry about that. They might even get a chance to learn about the people behind their food—people like Jessie and Mike Lane.

"I used to order grilled cheese wherever we'd go," says Jessie Lane. But things have changed since she married a lobsterman. "Once I started trying things that came off the boat," she continues, "it was a whole new world." In addition to fresh lobster and scallops still twitching in their shells, there's the produce, bread, and other food Lane gets in trade from other vendors at the farmers' markets where she sells the family's catch.

Lane and her husband, Mike, live south of Boston in Scituate, where they both grew up and where Mike's father is also a lobsterman. The Lanes work as a team, with Mike on the water and Jessie selling the lobster at farmers' markets on the South Shore. They started five years ago, at one point selling at six markets a week—including Winchester, where Jessie Lane met Chris Parsons.

Although Massachusetts has long had an abundance of markets for a state its size, seeing fresh fish vendors at market was rare. But in 2008 when the economy was failing, the lobster industry took a hard hit, and prices dropped to some of their lowest levels in years. The Lanes felt lucky they'd already decided to give the farmers' market route a try, where direct sales give them a much more stable price than the wholesale market offers.

It's more work, admits Jessie, but they don't mind. Being a market vendor gives her the flexibility she needs while raising two young kids. "They love coming with me to the market," she says, "and it teaches them good lessons too." And exposes them to a world of food beyond grilled cheese.

Lane's Lobster Salad
with Charred Corn and Heirloom Tomatoes

Serves 6

1 bunch basil, removed from stems and rough chopped
1/4 c. lime juice
1/4 c. Chardonnay vinegar
1 c. extra virgin olive oil
3 1-lb. local lobsters, cooked, cooled, and removed from shell, tails cut in half
3 heirloom tomatoes, sliced and seasoned with salt, black pepper, and a splash of extra virgin olive oil
2 avocados, halved, seed and skin removed, flesh cubed
2 ears corn, charred on the grill and kernels removed from the cob
kosher salt and cracked black pepper
fleur de sel

Whisk together the basil, lime juice, vinegar, and olive oil and season with kosher salt to taste. Place the lobster meat, avocado, and charred corn in a medium-sized bowl and spoon some basil vinaigrette over the mixture. Season with kosher salt and cracked black pepper and stir to combine. There should be an even coating of vinaigrette, but it shouldn't be soupy. Fan the marinating heirloom tomatoes on a large plate and arrange the lobster salad over the tomatoes. Sprinkle with fleur de sel and cracked black pepper and serve.

Tomato

Wild tomatoes are native to western South America from Ecuador to the Galapagos Islands, according to the U.S. Department of Agriculture. Mexico and Peru both have legitimate claims to the tomato's earliest domestication, but in any case it did not appear in Europe until the sixteenth century. At that time, Europeans grew tomatoes strictly as ornamental plants. The fruit was thought to be poisonous.

The best tomatoes, of course, come out of the garden, being heirloom varieties such as Brandywine and Mortgage Lifter that are prized more for their flavor than for their durability or shelf life. Most gardeners say let tomatoes ripen on the vine, but the experts at Texas A&M University (they grow a lot of tomatoes in Texas) say you'll get just as much flavor from a tomato picked at first sign of color and left to ripen at room temperature. More importantly, the birds will get none of it.

Smoked Tomato Gazpacho
with Lane's Lobster, Avocado, and Cilantro

Serves 6

You will need a stovetop smoker for this recipe.

8 ripe summer tomatoes, quartered
1 red onion, quartered
1 red pepper, seeded and quartered
10 sprigs cilantro
2 c. grilled sourdough bread, cubed
1 c. extra virgin olive oil
1/4 c. Sherry vinegar
1/4 c. Cabernet vinegar
kosher salt and cracked black pepper
extra virgin olive oil, for sprinkling
2 tbsp. chives, minced
3 1-lb. local lobsters, cooked, cooled, and removed from shell,
   cut into 1/2-inch pieces
juice of three limes
1 tbsp. extra virgin olive oil
2 avocadoes, removed from skin, seed discarded, cut into
   1/2-inch dice
small bunch baby cilantro
2 tsp. fleur de sel
6 grilled sourdough toast points

Place six of the quartered tomatoes, the red onion, and the red pepper in a stovetop smoker and smoke with applewood for 20 minutes. Remove vegetables from the smoker and cool.

Place the cooled smoked vegetables in a blender with the remaining tomatoes, cilantro, grilled bread, olive oil, Sherry, and Cabernet vinegar. Blend until smooth and strain through a fine sieve. Season with kosher salt and chill.

Ladle the soup into six bowls and sprinkle with extra virgin olive oil, cracked pepper, and chives. In a medium-sized bowl, gently mix the lobster, lime juice, olive oil, avocado, cilantro, and fleur de sel. Serve family style with the sourdough toast points on the side.

Rendezvous

Chef Steve Johnson
Eva's Garden

If it's summertime, and Steve Johnson isn't cooking, overseeing service, or tending to his rooftop garden at Rendezvous—his laid-back restaurant in Central Square, Cambridge—chances are he's hanging out on *Blue Sky*, his houseboat on the Westport River.

Westport, in the southeastern corner of Massachusetts, is one of the state's most prolific farming and fishing communities, and home to a handful of farmers whose produce appears on restaurant menus all over Boston. Johnson takes advantage of his proximity to these resources when he's down there, visiting farm stands and markets, digging shellfish, and fishing. The meals he cooks aboard *Blue Sky*—with a tiny propane stove and grill—are studies in simple, seasonal food.

At Rendezvous, Johnson's food is similarly pared down. The style is influenced by Western Mediterranean and North African flavors and techniques. As a graduate student in French literature in the 1970s, Johnson spent four years in southwestern France, where his introduction to the seasonal, market-based food sensibility changed his career path. Rather than return to academia, Johnson got a job in a restaurant when he returned to the United States.

"I spent the better part of fifteen to twenty years retroactively learning, by cooking in restaurants, about the sensibility I was introduced to in France," says the self-trained chef. "I read cookbooks and selected my jobs carefully."

Arriving in Boston in 1988, Johnson went to work for Gordon Hamersley, another self-trained chef whose travels to France inspired him to open his own place. At the time, says Johnson, Boston's farm-to-table dining scene was just gearing up. "There was no planning, no organization, no ordering," he says. "Farmers literally showed up at the back door of the restaurant."

Johnson has long cultivated relationships with farmers and based his food on New England's seasonal foods. He keeps a rooftop garden at the restaurant, where he raises herbs like rosemary, chervil, and lovage—practically year-round.

Where he has the most fun, and the most luck, is with fish and shellfish. "There are all of these dire predictions regarding marine resources, but this part has always been easy for me. I feature squid from Rhode Island fifty-two weeks a year, for example." he says, "Maybe [it's easy] because I spend time on the water, talk to others who know more than I do." As a fisherman, says Johnson, he's also attuned to seasonality and works his menus accordingly. In the summertime in Westport, he digs for clams and fishes for crabs and fluke, and his menus in Cambridge feature other local gems like bluefish and striped bass.

Before Johnson was growing most of his own herbs on top of the restaurant, longtime friend and farmer Eva Sommaripa, based in South Dartmouth (next to Westport), was a source of both produce and knowledge. "I've learned a lot from her over the years," says Johnson.

Whether it's a root, a bulb, a stem, a flower, a leaf, or a seed, Eva Sommaripa can tell you what that plant part is good for. These days, she says, she's excited by edible invasive species like the Japanese knotweed and autumn olives she's been gathering from the woods around her farm and experimenting with in her kitchen.

Eva has been providing high-end Boston-area restaurants with specialty herbs and vegetables from her farm for more than thirty years. If you've eaten at fine dining restaurants in Greater Boston during this time, she has likely expanded your palate. From knotweed to calamint to sweet cicely, goosefoot, and purslane, her niche is the uncommon (but delicious).

Sommaripa arrived in South Dartmouth by accident, having landed in nearby Providence to study pottery at the Rhode Island School of Design in 1965. Visiting friends in the area, she fell in love with the landscape, she says. "I loved the proximity to oceans and salt marshes, whatever it was—it just hit." She built a pottery cabin on her friends' property and started spending weekends there. A couple of years later, the property was for sale, and she and her husband George bought it. "Now I can hardly tear myself away," she says. She farms two of her twenty-plus acres; the rest are woods.

Like Ben Maleson, the mushroom forager, and Pat Woodbury, the shellfish farmer, Eva is integral in Boston's farm-to-chef network, having watched the development of ingredient-driven restaurants unfold before her, along with the corresponding growth in farmers' markets and community supported agriculture. For many chefs, Sommaripa has played a big role in their own understanding of uncommon plants and flavors.

"Eva was a living education in herbs," says Kevin Long, executive chef at Tosca restaurant in Hingham. "Wild edibles, lesser known European herbs; always the freshest and the best. Crazy stuff nobody has ever used or even heard of: elderflowers, miner's lettuce—she exposed us to it and we learned how to use it, sell it, market it, and educate our staff about it."

Don't be surprised when Japanese knotweed starts showing up on menus all over town. That's Eva.

Turkish Tomato Salad

Serves 4

Tomatoes and cucumbers are mixed frequently in Turkish cooking, and black olives and goat's milk cheese are used often as well. I use goat's milk feta in this dish because it is tangier and less salty than most sheep's milk fetas. Marjoram (substitute oregano if necessary) and mint are regular summer herbs used in this part of the world, and maras pepper is a paprika-level dried spice native to eastern Turkey. The salad can be prepared ahead of time, and the results are even better because of it.

2 lbs. mixed heirloom tomatoes, rinsed

1 cucumber, rinsed (peeling optional)

1/4 tsp. maras pepper

1–2 tbsp. Red Wine Vinaigrette (recipe follows)

12 kalamata (or similar) olives, pitted and roughly chopped

1/2 c. goat's milk feta cheese

1 tbsp. fresh flat leaf parsley, chopped

1 tsp. fresh mint, chopped

1 tsp. fresh marjoram, chopped

kosher salt and cracked black pepper

One hour before serving, slice the tomatoes 1/2 inch thick and the cucumber 1/8 inch thick and arrange on a serving platter. Season the tomatoes and cucumber lightly with salt and pepper, and then sprinkle the maras pepper over as well. Drizzle a small amount of the vinaigrette over the vegetables. Scatter the chopped olives and crumble the feta cheese on top as well.

Let the salad stand until ready to serve. When ready, drizzle more vinaigrette on top if desired and then scatter the fresh herbs equally around just prior to serving.

RED WINE VINAIGRETTE:

1 c. red wine vinegar

4 shallots, peeled and sliced thin

1 tbsp. Dijon mustard

2 tsp. fresh thyme leaf

2 c. extra virgin olive oil

1 c. canola oil

kosher salt and ground black pepper

In a medium-sized mixing bowl, whisk together briefly the vinegar, shallot, mustard, and thyme. Slowly whisk in the oils and season to taste with salt and pepper.

Grilled Mackerel
with Vietnamese Cucumber Salad

Serves 4

This preparation takes advantage of a delicious and abundant local resource: the Boston mackerel that swim along the coast of New England. I like to grill them whole, which gives you the benefit of the extra flavor and moisture this technique provides.

The cucumber salad is inspired by a traditional Vietnamese accompaniment for grilled fish and can be used also with blue-fish, salmon, etc. It has the unique feature of being moderately spicy yet cool and refreshing at the same time—perfect for summertime dining.

4 medium-sized mackerel
olive oil
kosher salt
Vietnamese Cucumber Salad (see recipe below)

Prepare a moderately hot charcoal fire. Brush four medium-sized mackerel lightly with good olive oil and sprinkle with kosher salt. Grill them on each side for about 4–5 minutes. When properly cooked, the flesh comes easily off the bone. I always cook jasmine rice with minced ginger to go along with this.

* Note: Only buy super-fresh mackerel, whole fish intact, the same day you plan to use them. Ask the fishmonger to scale and gut them for you. I recommend one fish per person.

VIETNAMESE CUCUMBER SALAD:
1 small red onion (or 2 large shallots), peeled and sliced thin lengthwise
1 c. lime juice
1/4 c. sugar
2 tbsp. sambal oelek (chili garlic sauce)
2 tbsp. salt
1 tsp. nuoc cham (fish sauce)
1 cucumber
2 tbsp. cilantro, chopped
2 tbsp. mint, chopped

Mix the onion, lime juice, sugar, chili-garlic sauce, salt, and fish sauce together separately and allow to marinate for 2 hours. Peel, seed, and slice the cucumber into quarter-rounds 1/4-inch thick. Set aside.

Half an hour before serving, mix together the cucumbers and the marinated onions. At the moment of service add the fresh herbs, reserving a few to shower on top of the salad. Serve cool with the grilled mackerel and a few cut lime wedges.

Mackerel

Most know mackerel as a fish that has been preserved in one way or another—salted, smoked, or canned. The canned variety, according to a 2008 *Wall Street Journal* article, quickly became a proxy currency in United States federal prisons after cigarettes were banned.

Fresh mackerel is a different fish altogether. Meaty like swordfish and oily like salmon, mackerel can stand up to bold flavors, and it thrives in the heat of the grill or the searing skillet. If you're eating mackerel in the summer, it's probably caught in the Gulf of Maine, according to the Northeast Fisheries Science Center. Historically, the New England mackerel fleet sailed fast schooners equipped with specialized purse seine gear, and much of the modern Canadian fleet still uses purse seines. The fast-growing mackerel are considered sustainable and not very vulnerable to overfishing.

Lumiere

Chef Michael Leviton
Frizzell Hill Farm

"The food I cook is not about reinventing the wheel and pushing the culinary envelope," says Michael Leviton. "It's about cooking really good food, night in, night out." It's what he's been doing for more than a decade at Lumiere, the warm, sophisticated restaurant he owns just west of Boston in Newton, where Leviton grew up.

As much as any chef in the Boston area, Leviton works with local farmers, fishers, and producers he knows and trusts. His network of suppliers is deep—at this point, he says, producers come to him because he's built his reputation on supporting people who grow, raise, and catch exquisite, high-quality food. Without the efforts of dozens of producers, Lumiere would be much less of a restaurant, according to its chef.

Growing up in the Boston suburbs, Leviton washed dishes and prepped at local delis and sandwich shops—not the kind of work, he says, that would inspire a career in food. But during college in Connecticut, he took a job as a line cook at a nearby restaurant. The chef didn't show up one day, Leviton remembers, and the next thing he knew, he and one other woman were learning how to work a line. "The learning curve was straight up," he says, "I was hooked." Within weeks of graduating from Wesleyan, Leviton headed west to San Francisco to pursue a cooking career.

Over the next eight years, Leviton worked and learned from people like Joyce Goldstein at Square One, Eric Ripert at Le Bernadin, and Daniel Boulud at Le Cirque. "I learned everything on the job," explains Leviton, "and read a ton. Every dollar I made went to dinner or cookbooks." With exposure to California's extravagant bounty of ingredients and a grounding in the regimentation of classic French technique, Leviton returned to New England for an executive chef position and opened Lumiere three years later, in 1999.

"I take pride in being here and being from New England," says Leviton. As much as he's able, Leviton supports the region's agricultural and fishing communities. Because he has built a reputation with both producers and diners, Leviton is able to take chances on producers. "I can make choices based on my desire to see someone succeed—it's better for all of us down the road if they do succeed."

And because Leviton has become a go-to chef for so many producers—helping them improve and refine their products—he's able to get unique ingredients that most people don't have access to. "Some of the really cool product that we're getting, you don't really get at a retail level," he says. "It's a lot of fun to have access to these things. It's what makes it exciting."

Take, for example, the goats he's been buying from Lynette Snedeker, a part-time farmer in western Massachusetts. Snedeker, a music teacher, grew up on a dairy farm in southeastern Pennsylvania. Her grandparents, parents, and siblings were all farmers. "Farming is part of who I am," she says. "But I knew I didn't want to be a farmer."

Instead, Snedeker studied music at the University of Hartford, where she met her husband. When the couple, both animal lovers, bought their now sixty-acre property in Leyden in 1996, they also bought two horses to keep as pets. In 2007, Snedeker, tired of constantly clearing land for the horses, added twelve goats to the mix to help keep the land clear. She now has forty breeding stock goats on the farm, along with one buck.

"It just makes sense," says Snedeker, whose day job is as the elementary school band teacher for the Pioneer Valley regional school system. "Goats are browsers—they eat everything—poison ivy, hemlocks, pine needles, bark." The goats have helped keep the land clear, but they've recently started bringing in a side income too. "We knew that if we were going to bring in animals, it would need to be profitable," she says. Snedeker wasn't interested in raising the goats for milk, having learned as a kid how closely dairying ties you to the farm.

Instead, she raises her Boer, Cashmere, and Nubian breeds for meat and sells them to a few chefs in the Boston area, including Leviton. Working with the chefs is a good fit, says Snedeker, because she knows where the animals are headed and that they'll be treated respectfully. "[Leviton] takes them whole and uses every bit," she explains. "Growing up on a farm, we always slaughtered our own animals, so I really appreciate that. It's ethical."

Miso-Glazed Bluefish with Baby Beets, Swiss Chard, and Oranges

Serves 4

3 bunches baby gold or chiogga beets
1/2 c. (approximately) seasoned rice vinegar (look for
  Marukan brand)
1/2 c. (approximately) water
1 bunch green Swiss chard, ribs removed, cut into 1-inch
  squares, washed, and drained
1 orange
1 tbsp. extra virgin olive oil
4 6-oz. bluefish fillets, skinned and pin bones removed
Miso Mustard Glaze (recipe follows)
lemon juice
Meyer Lemon Vinaigrette (recipe follows)

Set the oven to 400 degrees. Cut the tops and bottoms off of the beets and wash them under cold water. Place the beets in an oven-proof dish large enough to hold them in a single layer. Combine equal parts rice vinegar and water, enough to come to about half-way up the beets. Seal the vessel with a layer of foil, then plastic wrap, and then another layer of foil. Cook the beets in the oven for about 45 minutes or until they can be easily pierced with a knife. Peel the beets with a damp towel or under cold water. When cool, cut into fourths lengthwise.

With a small sharp knife, remove the top and bottom of the orange, cutting just below the skin and pith. Place the orange on one of the flat cut sides and pare down the sides of the orange, again cutting just below the pith. Try to remove all of the pith. Now cut the orange horizontally in 1/4-inch slices. Cut the slices into quarters and reserve.

In a medium-sized sauté pan, warm about 1 tbsp. olive oil and then add the beets. When warm, add the Swiss chard, mix well, and continue to cook until the chard begins to wilt. Set aside.

Season the fish with salt and pepper. Brush both sides of each fillet with the miso glaze. Heat a nonstick pan over high heat. Add the fish flesh-side down and cook for about 2–3 minutes, until the miso just begins to caramelize and turn black. Flip the fish and place it in the oven for about 4–5 minutes, until barely done. Remove the pan from the oven and let the fish rest in the pan for 1 minute. Squeeze a bit of lemon juice over the fish and then remove it from the pan.

Toss the vegetable mixture over medium heat to warm through. Add the orange sections and season with salt and freshly ground pepper. Place one quarter of the vegetable mixture in the center of each of four plates. Top with the fish and (artfully) spoon about 2 tbsp. of the vinaigrette over and around the fish. Serve.

MISO MUSTARD GLAZE:

- 1 c. red miso
- 1/2 c. mirin
- 1/2 c. canola oil
- 1/4 c. Dijon mustard

Combine all of the ingredients in a food processor and blend until the mixture is homogeneous.

MEYER LEMON VINAIGRETTE:

- 1 1/2 tsp. Dijon mustard
- 1 tsp. seasoned rice vinegar
- 3 tsp. Meyer lemon juice
- 1 c. Meyer Lemon Oil (recipe follows)
- 1 c. extra virgin olive oil
- 1/3 c. chives, finely minced

Place the mustard in a mixing bowl with the vinegar and the lemon juice, whisk well. Slowly whisk in the two oils. Reserve. Just before serving the fish, add the chives to about 2/3 c. of the vinaigrette and mix gently.

MEYER LEMON OIL:

- 1/2 tsp. Meyer lemon zest, finely minced
- 9 oz. canola oil

Steep the zest in the oil by puréeing until warm and letting sit for at least 1 hour. Strain through a filter. Yield should be about 1 c.

Bluefish

Aggressive, migratory, and delicious, bluefish are a favorite among recreational fishermen and fish-loving cooks. *Pomatomus salatrix* are found in waters all over the world, but in New England, large schools migrate to our waters in the summertime. Known for their rich, meaty flavor, bluefish are best when super-fresh, before the oils in their flesh have a chance to make the fillets taste "fishy." Their robust flavor and dense texture hold up well on the grill or when broiled, and with assertive sauces or accompaniments.

fall

In the dead of winter when the world is frozen, people in New England ask each other why we live here. From the perspective of seasonal eating, fall might be the answer. As creative cooks use the season's bounty to swap out the simple preparations of summer for cool-weather cooking's more complex techniques and layers of flavor, thousands of university students return to town, the arts season gets underway, and, if we're lucky, the Red Sox continue to play. Enough to make you forget how quickly winter follows.

Hungry Mother

Chef Barry Maiden

Woodbury Shellfish

The first time Barry Maiden left the South was to attend culinary school in Vermont at age twenty-three. While he was enrolled at the New England Culinary Institute in Montpelier, he got an internship at L'Espalier, a fine dining institution in Boston's Back Bay that has seen dozens of Boston's best cooks come through its kitchens.

"When I walked up to that big iron gate," says Maiden, "I had butterflies." L'Espalier was located in an old townhouse at the time, with a brick façade and narrow, curving stairs leading up to the dining rooms. "I hit the buzzer—I was so scared," he continues, "and I remember walking up all those steps, all the way up to the top in the kitchen."

The attention to detail and technique in L'Espalier's kitchen was critical training for Maiden. Chef/owner Frank McClelland "takes it a step further than most chefs," says Maiden, who continued on at the restaurant when his internship ended, eventually helping to open McClelland's more relaxed bistro, Sel de la Terre, on the waterfront in 2000.

Working in kitchens focused on technique and ingredients was part of Maiden's plan at that point in his career, but it was a long way from where he got his start cooking in his hometown of Abingdon, Virginia, in the southwest corner of the state. While Sunday suppers at Grandma's house were part of life growing up, he didn't have longstanding plans to become a chef. "I got into cooking to get a job," he says. "I worked at Shoney's, on the grill and the fryer. I got to hang out with my friends—it was fun." One cooking job led to another, and Maiden learned the trade from the ground up, washing dishes and peeling shrimp before he mastered working on the line. Next thing he knew, he was Vermont-bound.

Less than a decade later at his Cambridge restaurant, Hungry Mother, where he is one of four owners, Maiden's very personal culinary sensibility comes through—southern Appalachian food interpreted through French technique and New England ingredients. It's a style that was incubated in culinary school, he says, where an instructor once told him, "Your food's good, but something's missing. It's missing you."

Boiled peanuts, pimento cheese, chicken and dumplings—the restaurant's menu seems like a list of the chef's favorite foods, all made with ingredients sourced from producers Maiden gets to know. When building his ever-expanding menu of suppliers, says the chef, "I try to go direct as much as I can." Most of the produce is locally grown, but many ingredients, like sorghum and peanuts, are brought up from the South. No matter how far the ingredients travel, Maiden makes a point of working with family farmers and producers. "I like to have a conversation with the people," he explains. "How's life? How's business? That kind of thing."

As Maiden's supplier network expands, so does his commitment to working this way. Menus are reprinted daily to reflect new ingredients walking in the door. It's exciting. "In one sense, it makes my head spin," he says. "But I also love stocking my walk-in with beautiful produce I don't have a plan for."

One of the producers Maiden works with directly is Pat Woodbury. Scan almost any good restaurant menu in Boston, and you'll see them: Pat's clams. When Woodbury and his wife, Barbara, started their shellfish farm in Wellfleet on Cape Cod twenty-five years ago, they had no idea they'd be on the leading edge of a curve trending toward local, seasonal, directly marketed ingredients.

As grad students at the University of Chicago studying marine science in the mid-1980s, Woodbury isn't sure what made him and Barbara decide to move to Cape Cod and try their hands at an industry that was only about ten years old at the time. "What was the logical jump, I don't know," Woodbury says, "but we decided to head to Wellfleet and give [shellfish farming] a try."

They arrived when the restaurant scene in Boston was, as he puts it, exploding. "So we just started knocking on doors in restaurants," he says. "We developed one customer at a time—it was all about connecting with chefs who wanted to work direct with producers. Word of mouth got around."

While Cape Cod's unique coastal geography has made it a productive area for shellfish for hundreds of years, aquaculture has only been introduced more recently. It's been a great thing, from both an ecological and a taste perspective.

Like farmers on land, the Woodburys plant a new crop of clam seeds every year. The clams take two to three years to reach maturity, and during that time, they do their part to filter the water they grow in as they eat. Their diet of phytoplankton also means that no feed is introduced to the shellfish beds, which reduces the overall impact on the cultivated areas.

The clams and oysters raised around Wellfleet have specific flavor profiles that reflect the time of year they're harvested, their diet of phytoplankton, and the tidal shifts of the areas where they grow. It's the aquatic version of *terroir*, or the taste of place, according to some shellfish farmers. "With the flavor component," says Woodbury, "the seasonal variations and variations from site to site are pretty startling."

Those varied, startling flavor profiles are part of what chefs love about working with the Woodburys. Their business has grown apace with the shellfish aquaculture industry and Boston chefs' interest in buying local food directly from producers. "It's been a natural progression," says Woodbury. "As the food movement grew in Boston, we grew with it."

Grilled Clams with Country Ham, Pickled Butternut Squash, and Tabasco Mayonnaise

Serves 4–6 as a first course

4 oz. (about a scant cup) thinly sliced country-style Virginia ham, julienned

24 middle- or topneck-sized clams, scrubbed and cleaned of any sand (no need to purge)

1/2 c. Tabasco Mayonnaise (recipe follows)

1/4 c. Pickled Butternut Squash, thinly sliced or minced (recipe follows)

chopped fresh chives, for garnish

Prepare a hot grill, preferably charcoal to help impart some smokiness to the clams. Place a heavy-bottomed sauté pan over medium heat and add the ham. Stir constantly with a wooden spoon to help the ham cook evenly (this will also help the ham separate as it cooks). Continue cooking until ham is browned and crispy (about 3 minutes). Remove immediately with a slotted spoon to a paper towel and allow to drain and cool. (This can be done well in advance.)

Place clams flat on the hot side of the grill, directly on the grill grate. Cover and cook until they pop open (3–5 minutes). Be careful to pull the clams off before all the juice is lost to the grill. Use tongs to transfer clams and their juices to a plate or platter. (Discard any that do not open.) You may remove the top half of the opened clam shell at this point for easier eating.

Top with a dollop of Tabasco Mayonnaise, bits of crispy country ham, and slices of Pickled Butternut Squash. Garnish with fresh-cut chives. Serve while still warm.

TABASCO MAYONNAISE (YIELD: APPROXIMATELY 1 1/2 CUPS):

1 egg yolk

1/2 tbsp. Dijon mustard

1 tbsp. fresh-squeezed lemon juice

3/4 tbsp. rice wine or cider vinegar

1/2 tsp. fine sea salt

1 1/4 c. canola or safflower oil

2 tsp. Tabasco sauce

Combine egg yolk, Dijon mustard, lemon juice, vinegar, and sea salt in a small mixing bowl. Whisking constantly, slowly add the oil in a slow, thin, steady stream until it is completely incorporated. The mayonnaise should look creamy and emulsified at this point. Whisk in the Tabasco. Refrigerate until ready to use.

PICKLED BUTTERNUT SQUASH
(YIELD: 3–4 CUPS—MUCH MORE THAN YOU WILL NEED):

1 large butternut squash, peeled and cut into 3/4-inch cubes

1 1/2 tbsp. kosher salt

8 fresh sage leaves

1 2/3 c. cider vinegar

2/3 c. brown sugar

3/4 c. apple cider

In a large bowl, toss peeled and cubed squash with salt and let sit for 4 hours. Strain and discard liquid from squash.

Combine remaining ingredients and bring to a boil. Reduce heat, add squash to hot pickle liquid, and continue to simmer until squash is just tender (about 15 minutes). Remove from heat and let stand at room temperature for 2 hours, then refrigerate.

Apples

Apples are thought to have originated in Kazakhstan, on the Asian steppe, but nowhere has the fruit been so thoroughly grafted onto a nation's identity than in America today. The first waves of European settlers here relied on the apple to make hard cider, sweet cider, and cider vinegar. No less a folkloric figure than Johnny Appleseed was known for planting cider orchards, as Michael Pollan points out in his book, *The Botany of Desire*.

Two hundred years later, cider is no longer so widely consumed, but apples are still a favorite in any number of preparations. The steamed apple cake presented here is probably as American as any other after-dinner sweet—but it wouldn't do it justice to compare it to apple pie, now would it?

Steamed Apple Pudding Cake
with Applesauce

Serves 6–8

PUDDING CAKE:

- nonstick pan spray
- 4–5 tbsp. sorghum
- 1 c. plus 3 tbsp. all-purpose flour
- 1 tsp. salt
- 1 tsp. baking powder
- 3/4 c. unsalted butter, at room temperature
- 1 c. plus 1 tbsp. sugar
- 3 large eggs, at room temperature
- 1 c. apples, peeled and diced in 1-inch cubes (Cortlands would work here)

Preheat the oven to 350 degrees. Have a deep baking dish and a bundt pan ready. Coat the bundt pan with nonstick spray and sprinkle the sorghum on the bottom of the pan to coat the surface. In a large mixing bowl, sift together the flour, salt, and baking powder. Set aside.

In a standing mixer fitted with the paddle attachment, cream the butter and sugar on medium speed until pale and fluffy (about 3 minutes). Add the eggs, one at a time, scraping down the sides of the bowl in between. Reduce the speed to low and add the dry ingredients. Mix just until combined. Fold in the diced apples, mixing gently. Pour the batter into the bundt pan, place the bundt pan in the deep baking dish, and fill the baking dish with warm water to come halfway up the side of the bundt pan.

Bake for 1 hour or until the cake has risen and is springy to the touch. Remove from the oven and set aside to cool for 10 minutes. Invert onto a serving plate. Serve with lightly sweetened whipped cream and applesauce.

APPLESAUCE:

- 4 medium Cortland or Macintosh apples, red skin left on
- 2 tbsp. sugar
- 1 vanilla pod
- juice of 2 lemons

Roughly chop the apples. Add them to a small saucepan, along with the sugar, vanilla, lemon juice, and a splash of water. Bring to a simmer and cook over medium-low heat gently until the apples are soft. Remove from the heat and discard the vanilla pod. Blend the sauce in a food processor or with an immersion blender. Pass it through a fine mesh strainer.

Erbaluce

Chef Charles Draghi

Ben's Mushrooms

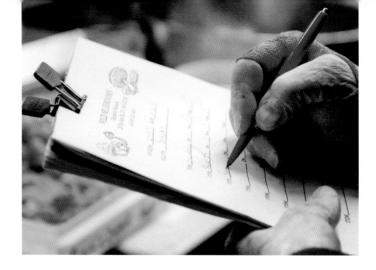

"I'm a flavor guy," says Charles Draghi. Draghi's fifty-seat restaurant, Erbaluce, is around the corner from the Copley Square market, where he shops every Tuesday and Friday for the restaurant's produce. "I like the gnarly, knobby stuff," he says, pointing out celeriac and odd-shaped carrots as he wanders through the market stalls.

No matter what his raw ingredients look like, Draghi sees his job as bringing out their true nature. It's his culinary style, which is influenced by growing up in Windsor, Connecticut, with Italian aunts who "grew everything they could" and spending summers as boy in Italy's Piedmont region, where his family originated. "Italian food is extremely regional," he says, "and all about ingredients."

Though Draghi's been rolling gnocchi since he was six, his formal culinary training began as a young cook at 1980s fine dining destination L'Americain in Hartford, Connecticut. He moved to Boston in 1986, working at L'Espalier under Moncef Meddeb, and later resuscitated North End restaurant Marcuccio's from a dime-a-dozen red sauce joint to a regional Italian standout among spaghetti parlors.

After parting ways with Marcuccio's owner, Draghi bounced around Boston on the lookout for his own place, taking different consulting chef positions and working for five years in the front of the house for Barbara Lynch at No. 9 Park.

When Erbaluce, named after a little-known northern Italian wine grape, opened in 2008, Draghi was free to refine his style, which he describes as straddling the sensibilities of food-as-craft and food-as-art. "If you are served a plate that I have cooked, you can easily identify it as mine," he says. For example, two signatures in his repertoire—seared matsutake mushrooms with taleggio cheese and arugula, or rack of wild boar with fermented Concord grape sauce—appear regularly on the always-changing menu.

One of the ways Draghi chases flavor seems counterintuitive. He doesn't use any butter in his savory cooking, instead favoring herbs and infusions to build layers of flavor in his dishes. "Butter masks flavor," he explains. For many people, tasting restaurant food that's been liberated from copious amounts of fat and salt can be jarring, but they usually come around.

The key to his pursuit of flavor, Draghi says, is in what he does outside the kitchen, building his network of suppliers and bringing in the highest-quality ingredients he can find. According to the chef, New England is as much an inspiration as Italy, and "no place in the world has the variety and quality of fish" produced in the deep, cold waters off of the New England coast. Draghi draws parallels between the geography of New England and parts of Italy, with the range of topography represented in such a small space. But in either place, such geography makes for great ingredients. "The quality and variety of food that can be grown in New England is as good as anywhere in the world."

That includes the wild mushrooms. Anyone who's worked in fine dining restaurants in Boston has probably encountered Ben Maleson, also known as Ben the Mushroom Man. With his white beard and long, braided hair covered with a floppy leather hat, Maleson looks the part of someone who's been selling mushrooms to Boston restaurants for more than thirty years. He got his start selling to the old Upstairs at the Pudding (now down the street and called Upstairs on the Square) and currently has about thirty accounts with restaurants like TW Food, L'Espalier, and Erbaluce.

Although there's potential to expand further, "I have to connect on a personal basis," he says. "It puts me in a relationship with a lot of chef-owners—people with a lot of hands-on involvement with the food they're producing. I've been working with the same kind of people for thirty years, people with the creativity, with the interest to try something and present something new."

Maleson grew up in Newton, where he started identifying and picking mushrooms as a boy. Encouraged by his mother, family friends, and other adults who fostered his interest in science and nature, Maleson became engrossed in his hobby. He'd pick mushrooms on the way home from school, take them home, and cook them as a snack.

One day a friend looked at Maleson and his clutch of porcini mushrooms and said, "You shouldn't eat those." Maleson was puzzled. "You should sell them," his friend said. They went to a restaurant on Beacon Hill, says Maleson, and sold two big porcini mushrooms for $50. His career developed from there.

Early on, Maleson made deliveries by subway. Over time, his business grew through word of mouth and with the web of cooks moving from restaurant to restaurant around town. He now deals with wild mushrooms he's foraged himself, mushrooms foraged by gatherers he knows all over the world, and cultivated mushrooms, both domestic or imported.

Although now some of the more common wild mushrooms are available to chefs through other suppliers, few suppliers have Maleson's national network of foragers who find the rare, seasonal mushrooms and hold them for him. "Because I have the relationship with people, and I have the knowledge of the mushrooms, I can get really unique things," he says. "I know the mushrooms, I know the people, and I encourage [the industry's development]."

Matsutake Salad with Taleggio

Serves 2

You need a propane torch or a very hot broiler for this recipe.

1 1-oz. piece taleggio cheese, cut into 2 pieces
1 large matsutake mushroom (about 3 oz., or the size of a
  small portabello mushroom), brushed clean and thinly sliced
2 c. sylvetta (wild Italian arugula) or organic baby arugula
1 tbsp. basil, chopped
1 tbsp. mint, chopped
1 lemon wedge
1 tbsp. extra virgin olive oil
sea salt and freshly ground white pepper

With the back of a spoon, smear each piece of taleggio across a salad plate to create a thin coating on the bottom of the two plates. Arrange the matsutake slices across the taleggio coating, and, using the propane torch, char the edges and gills of the mushroom slices.

In a medium-sized bowl, mix the arugula, the chopped herbs, a squeeze of lemon, and the olive oil, and season with salt and pepper to taste. Arrange the dressed arugula onto the salad plates on top of the mushroom slices. Serve with a crisp, minerally white wine and some garlic toast.

Wild Mushrooms

Unless you've learned enough about mushrooms to forage with confidence, most home cooks don't come across the same variety of wild mushrooms as a chef who knows a wholesaling forager. Even most chefs don't get to experience the thousand or so types of edible fungi growing out there in the world; a few dozen will have to do. But mushrooms of all kinds—from the now-common cultivated shiitake to prized truffles and boletes—add distinctive flavor and aroma to any dish they're featured in. Up to 80 or 90 percent water, mushrooms have flavors that intensify when cooked—slow cooking over dry heat allows mushrooms to expel their water and concentrate the flavor and fragrance.

Roman Broccoli
with a Lemon-Herb Zabaglione

Serves 4 as a side dish or first course

3 egg yolks
1/8 tsp. nutmeg, freshly grated
1/4 tsp. anchovy fillet, finely minced
juice and zest from half a lemon (zest finely minced)
1/4 c. dry white wine
2 large sprigs each: sage, mint, parsley, and thyme, leaves
   removed and finely chopped, branches reserved
sea salt and freshly ground white pepper
1/3 c. extra virgin olive oil
1 head organic Roman broccoli, cut into small florettes
zest of 1/2 lemon, minced
additional nutmeg, freshly grated

In a double boiler, or in a medium-sized stainless steel mixing bowl placed over a saucepan of barely simmering water, whisk together the egg yolks, the nutmeg, the anchovy, half of the lemon juice, and all of the wine.

Whisk the yolks constantly until they cook slightly into a light, silky sauce with the consistency of a light mayonnaise, then remove the bowl from the heat, add the remaining lemon juice and chopped herbs, and continue to whisk periodically as the mixture cools down to room temperature. Season with salt and pepper to taste, and set the sauce (zabaglione) aside.

Add the olive oil to a large sauté pan over medium heat. When the oil shimmers, add the Roman broccoli and the herb branches. Sauté the broccoli until it is tender (about 7–10 minutes). Discard the herb branches and season the broccoli with salt and pepper to taste.

Remove the Roman broccoli to a serving dish and sauce with the zabaglione. Garnish with the lemon zest and some more herb sprigs. Add a light sprinkling of freshly grated nutmeg.

Eat Boston

Chef Will Gilson
The Herb Lyceum

Restaurant owner Karen Masterson is on a mission, and it concerns soup. Her restaurant, Nourish, strives to serve food that's both responsibly bought and reasonably priced. But it goes beyond that, she says. "I hope the food at Nourish will inspire people to get back into the kitchen," says Masterson. "There are not a lot of people who even have the confidence to make a pot of soup."

As a lifelong cook and gardener, gathering around home-grown, home-cooked meals has been central in Masterson's family life. She grew up in Alberta, Canada, making jam and shopping at farm stands with her mom. "I've always grown my own food, canned, and preserved food," she says. "That's what life has been for my kids and my family." It's a sensibility she tries to share at Nourish.

A neighborhood spot with a broad-ranging menu, Nourish strikes a balance between price and sourcing responsibly. Masterson has made a point of pricing the menu items at accessible, everyday-meal levels. "It's not chef-driven, not fine dining," she says. "I'm trying to welcome more people to the table." To save on labor and also support local food businesses, she brings in value-added products like spice blends and cranberry chutney. Her seafood comes from fisheries she knows are well-managed, and she's held special dinners with fishermen to help educate her diners about seafood sustainability. She buys produce locally when it's in season, she says, but can't afford to do everything. Grass-fed beef, for example, is offered in a meatloaf—ground beef is inexpensive compared to other cuts from a grass-fed steer.

Masterson is also able to keep prices down by offering vegetarian and vegan choices, like Thai curry or peanut-noodle stir-fry. She's not out to convert people, she says, but hopes that guests will begin to shift their sensibilities and see what else is possible when they're thinking about dinner. "A lot of people see tofu and tempeh on the menu and assume it's not for them," she explains. "But if you bring different tastes together at the table, maybe people will change the way they look at dinner."

One of the small producers Masterson works with is the New England Cranberry Company. In 2001, Allison Goldberg and Ted Stux were living in Chicago, expecting their first child, and looking to buy a business that would get them back to the East Coast where Allison had grown up. New England Cranberry was for sale online—Stux went out to see it, bought the business, and bought a house, and the couple took over the company right before their son was born.

A business best known for its chutneys and pepper jellies, New England Cranberry was purchased by Stux and Goldberg from a retired man who had started it as a hobby. Although the company is named for the iconic fruit of coastal New England, due to cost and a need for consistent availability, Stux and Goldberg look to other states like Michigan and Wisconsin for their berries.

While Goldberg and Stux do work with other producers and artisans in the region to create their products—maple syrup comes from farms in Massachusetts and New Hampshire, honey comes from an aviary in Maine, a chocolatier in Rhode Island makes their bark—they have a commitment to partnering locally whenever possible.

"When we bought it, the line consisted of six products in jars," Goldberg says. Since taking over, they have revamped the packaging and added dozens of new products, from organic iced tea and lemonade mixes to maple syrups and white chocolate–cranberry bark. "The brand loyalty is there," explains Goldberg, which allows them to experiment with new products. "Cranberries are still the main thing, but we're mixing it up."

Cauliflower-Kale Rolls

Cauliflower-Kale Rolls

Makes 6

olive oil
1 tbsp. garlic, peeled and minced fine
1 c. mushrooms, chopped into 1/2-inch pieces
1 c. kale, blanched, cooled, and finely chopped
1 c. caulifower, chopped into 1/2-inch pieces, blanched,
  and cooled
1/4 c. parsley, finely chopped
salt and pepper to taste
whole wheat phyllo pastry (follow package instructions)

Preheat the oven to 425 degrees. Grease a standard-sized cookie sheet and set aside. Place the olive oil in a large, heavy-bottomed skillet over medium heat. Add the garlic and cook, stirring gently, for 1 minute. Add the mushrooms and continue to cook until mushrooms are soft (about 8 minutes). Add the kale and the cauliflower and cook, stirring to combine all vegetables, until vegetables are all warmed through.

Unroll phyllo dough and cut one 11x18-inch sheet into thirds. Brush sheet with olive oil. Place 2 heaping tablespoons of cauliflower-kale mix along the bottom in the center of the sheet and roll up, folding in the sides after one full roll. Cut each roll in half. Brush with oil, place on a baking sheet, and bake for 10 minutes or until the rolls are browned and crisp. Serve with New England Cranberry Colonial Chutney.

Roasted Root Vegetable Soup

Serves 12

1/4 c. olive oil
3 c. butternut squash, chopped
2 c. carrots, chopped
1 1/2 c. parsnips, chopped
1 1/2 c. yellow turnips, chopped
1 c. leeks, chopped
2 c. onions, cut in chunks
8 c. vegetable stock
6 bay leaves
1 tbsp. fresh thyme leaves, chopped
2 tsp. fresh rosemary leaves, chopped
salt and pepper to taste
sour cream or crème fraîche

Set the oven to 350 degrees. In a large mixing bowl, toss the olive oil, squash, carrots, parsnips, turnips, leeks, and onions. Sprinkle with salt and pepper. Transfer to a large baking sheet (you may need two to keep from crowding the veggies) and place in the oven to roast. Roast for 25 minutes or until tender, turning occasionally to make sure they cook evenly.

Transfer to a large Dutch oven or soup pot on the stovetop and add stock. Raise the heat to high and bring to a boil. Reduce heat, add the bay leaves, thyme, and rosemary, and simmer for 10 minutes.

Purée with an immersion blender or transfer soup in small batches to a blender and purée until smooth. Adjust seasoning and serve garnished with a dollop of sour cream or crème fraîche.

Cranberries

Despite its saucy, tart reputation, the cranberry was embraced by early Puritan colonists in Massachusetts. Their whalers and merchant mariners used the cranberry to prevent scurvy, and the Pilgrims themselves gave the berry its English name. They thought the fruit's pink blossoms resembled the head of a Sandhill crane.

According to the Cape Cod Cranberry Growers' Association, the cranberry is one of only three North American native fruits that are commercially cultivated, with about forty thousand acres harvested each year. In Massachusetts, fourteen thousand acres are dedicated to cranberry production, but the mouth-puckering fruit is harvested from Delaware to Prince Edward Island. Seen by some people only once a year, next to turkey at Thanksgiving, the tart fruits are far more versatile than they get credit for—try them in muffins, pies, tarts, and turnovers as well as in chutneys and sauces.

Henrietta's Table

Chef Peter Davis

Sparrow Arc Farm

With dishes like red flannel hash, Yankee pot roast, and baked haddock on the menu at Henrietta's Table, there's no disputing Chef Peter Davis's New England bona fides. Known for his commitment to buying from local growers, Davis's food also features some of the region's humblest ingredients, such as dried beans, squashes, and all manner of tubers and roots. "I love things that grow underground," he says.

Davis, who grew up in Nahant with chickens and a garden in the backyard, caught the cooking bug from a friend's brother. During high school, he ran a pizza shop, working there six nights a week. Two days after graduation, he moved to upstate New York to attend the Culinary Institute of America with the intent of broadening his horizons and cooked his way down the East Coast, working in Virginia and Florida en route to the Virgin Islands. Eventually Davis took a position with the Hyatt in Singapore.

This was in the early 1980s, an exciting time in food, says Davis, when New American cuisine was emerging. In Singapore too, the quality of the food was eye-opening. "The cuisine I encountered in Asia was so simple," Davis explains. "Just a little oil, a really hot wok, and great vegetables."

"I was seeing new ingredients," he continues, "but also how important it was for produce to be fresh." Davis started thinking about one of his favorite restaurant models in the United States: the diner. "From a business perspective, diners are the restaurants that survive year after year—they're consistent, simple." Davis wondered how he could marry the basic comforts of a diner with the focus on fresh ingredients he'd encountered in Singapore.

After returning to the United States, Davis met Charles Hotel owner Dick Friedman, who had a vision of building a restaurant that reminded him of going to nearby Wilson Farms as a kid. At the time, there was nothing like it in the Boston area. Henrietta's Table, named for Friedman's pet pig he kept on Martha's Vineyard, opened in 1995. The hotel and restaurant have become known for supporting local producers, both with philanthropy and purchasing.

"Part of what's great for the growers is my buying power," says Davis, who integrates local ingredients into all aspects of dining at the hotel—from the restaurant to banquets and room service. He limits his vendor list but buys in high volume from the growers he works with. "I'm not going to work with a grower for $25 worth of vegetables."

For example, Davis buys in such high volume from Sparrow Arc Farm in Unity, Maine, that a few years ago, those sales enabled farm owner Matt Linehan to make his first purchase of his own land. Linehan focuses his business on wholesale accounts with chefs and restaurants from Portland, Maine, to New York City.

Linehan's focus on chefs is not least of all due to his affinity for that industry's culture. "Chefs and farmers are similar types of

people," says Linehan. "Both very passionate, heart on the sleeve, intense types of people."

Growing up in suburban Boston immersed in the punk rock scene, Linehan wanted to build his adult life outside the mainstream. After high school, he and a buddy enrolled in a farm training program called the Farm School in Athol, Massachusetts. Linehan didn't intend on starting an enterprise, however. "I thought I'd be homesteading," he says. "You know, growing the three sisters among the tree stumps."

It didn't take long before he caught the farming bug, though. "I realized I didn't want to grow food just for myself. I wanted to grow a lot of food—and give it away." His first position after attending the Farm School was as a grower at Lookout Farm in his hometown of Natick, and soon he moved north to Unity, Maine, to start his own farm.

Now in his seventh season, Linehan's focus is on artisan and heirloom vegetables. In many ways, chefs are the ideal market for heirlooms, says the farmer. Some heirlooms are exceptionally beautiful, others are funny-looking, some have remarkable flavors, but almost all have a unique story behind them, which chefs are very interested in.

Linehan's focus on selling to restaurants has yielded some satisfying partnerships. When working with chefs as opposed to selling at farmers' markets, he says, "you can have deeper relationships with fewer people."

Oven-Roasted Root Vegetables

Serves 4

2 small parsnips
1 small rutabaga, peeled
1 small purple-top turnip
1 small celeriac
2 small carrots
2 tbsp. unsalted butter, melted
salt and pepper

Preheat oven to 350 degrees. Have a flat-rimmed baking sheet ready. Cut all vegetables into 1-inch cubes. Place vegetables into a bowl and toss with the melted butter. Add salt and pepper to taste. Place on a flat baking tray, and roast for approximately 30 minutes, or until the vegetables are tender.

Maine Yellow Eye Beans
with Gilfeather Turnips

Serves 4–6

2 c. nitrate-free bacon, diced

2 medium yellow onions, cut into 1/2-inch dice

2 tsp. garlic, peeled and minced

1 jalapeño pepper, finely diced

10 c. chicken stock

2 c. Maine Yellow Eye beans, soaked overnight and drained

2 bay leaves

2 sprigs thyme

2 medium Gilfeather turnips, cut into 1/2-inch dice

salt and pepper

In a large, heavy-bottomed pot over medium heat, render the bacon. Add the onion, garlic, and jalapeño, and sauté until the onion is transparent (about 10 minutes). Add the chicken stock, beans, bay leaves, and thyme to the pot. Raise the heat to medium-high and bring to a boil. Reduce heat to a simmer and cook the beans until they are half-soft (about 30–40 minutes). Add in the turnip. Continue cooking until the beans are tender, another 30–40 minutes. Season with salt and pepper to taste, and serve.

Dried Beans

For such a humble ingredient, dried beans have a lot going for them. In the fields, they're a beneficial crop for enriching soil and attracting pollinators. In the kitchen, they have a dazzling variety of flavors, shapes, and colors—and they're an inexpensive, shelf-stable, and nutritious plant-based protein source too.

Beans have long been central to cuisines from Asia, Europe, and the Mediterranean to Central and South America. Their versatility is amazing: beans can be served hot or cold, in soups, stews, salads, dips, fritters, and more. Lentils, chickpeas, cannellini, and kidney are some of the most well-known common beans, but heirlooms, with names like Good Mother Stallard, Yellow Eye, and Jacob's Cattle, are worth experimenting with. These old-time varieties might even help beans catch on in American kitchens. There's hope!

Redd's in Rozzie

Chef Charlie Redd

Shack Foods

Anson Mills Farro Salad

Serves 4

1 tbsp. extra virgin olive oil
1 red onion, cut into 1/4-inch dice
2 cloves garlic, peeled and smashed
1 c. Anson Mills farro piccolo
1 fresh bay leaf
1 bunch kale, stemmed, blanched, and shocked in an ice bath
1 red onion
1–3 tbsp. spicy pickled peppers (any Latino food shop will have these)

Set the oven to 350 degrees. Place a medium-sized pot over medium heat. Add olive oil, and when it shimmers, add the onion, garlic, and bay leaf. Cook until aromatic and half-soft. Add the farro and cover with 2 1/2 c. water. Bring to a high simmer, cover, and reduce heat to low. Cook farro at a low simmer until done (about 30–45 minutes), adding water as necessary. You want to end up with the farro cooked and just a little cooking liquid left so as not to lose flavor.

Slice the red onion in half horizontally, and sear the cut side hard in a hot, heavy skillet until charred. Place the skillet in the oven and roast the onion until soft and toasty (about 20 minutes). When the onion is cool enough to handle, trim off both ends and discard. Pull the remaining onion apart into rings and set aside.

Mix farro, kale, chopped pickled peppers (to taste), and onion rings together and season with salt, pepper, parsley, and extra virgin olive oil if needed.

Rialto

Chef Jody Adams
Captain Marden's Seafood

"I can't remember a time I wasn't cooking," says Rialto chef-owner Jody Adams. Adams, celebrated for her regional Italian cuisine, grew up in a household where "being comfortable in a kitchen came early," she says.

Growing up in Providence, Rhode Island, Adams was one of three girls in a family where the dinner table was central in daily life. "My mom cooked everything from scratch," says Adams, "and she was adventurous—cooking from Elizabeth David, Julia Child, and *Gourmet*." This upbringing left Adams grounded not only in cooking but in a European-style sensibility of shopping at the market for the night's dinner. During high school and college, she assisted her neighbor, cookbook author and teacher Nancy Verde Barr, with cooking classes and recipe testing. Despite her experience with food, Adams never considered it as a profession, she says, "even though there I was, building this expertise and skill set and knowledge."

After studying anthropology at Brown University, Adams took a job at a gourmet shop in Tiverton, Rhode Island. Surrounded by the fresh-baked breads, jams and jellies, and imported cheeses, Adams says she realized, "I'm home. This is where I'm supposed to be."

Soon, Adams moved to Boston and established her culinary career working in some of Boston's most high-profile restaurants. Working under Lydia Shire, in the kitchen at Seasons in the Bostonian Hotel, introduced Adams to the possibility of working with New England ingredients using different techniques.

"Lydia's techniques ran the gamut," explains Adams, "from Chinese to Moroccan to Italian. But she was authentic in terms of what was on the plate." And when she helped Gordon Hamersley open his bistro, "the emphasis was on local ingredients, through the lens of French technique."

By the time Adams opened Rialto in 1994, four years of working as the executive chef at Michaela's had hooked her on regional Italian cooking. "I'm very interested in why a cuisine develops the way it does," she says. "Italy shows you that well."

Adams has long explored how geography influences cuisine, especially living in New England. "There's the idea of terroir," she says. "For example, when you think about Cape Cod, Maine, New Hampshire, Vermont, you think about food in very different ways." New England's constantly changing seasons inform her cooking. "We change the menu six times a year," she says, "because the season changes every two months."

Throughout her career, Adams has always bought from local farmers. "I've never claimed to be a locavore or to use only organics," she says, "but it's always been part of what I do. It's not just about carbon footprint, it's about building community. The depth of a connection to the food makes a huge difference for my staff, and they feel connected and passionate about it, and all of that is good."

Part of Boston's restaurant community for decades, Captain Marden's Seafood started out as a retail store in West Newton in the 1940s and moved to Wellesley in 1961. When third-generation owner Kim Marden graduated from college in 1980, he returned to the company to build the wholesale business. More than thirty years and three hundred wholesale accounts later, Captain Marden's is a household name in Greater Boston's restaurant world.

In that time, the seafood industry has changed dramatically. Many wild-caught fisheries, especially in New England, are under strict regulations to help fish populations rebound from overfishing. These regulations have shrunk the fishing fleet, put fishermen out of business, and driven up the cost of much of the wild-caught seafood that remains on the market.

At the same time, aquaculture has been on the rise and now accounts for over half of the global supply of seafood. As Captain Marden's has grown, the company has embraced aquaculture but continues to focus on selling New England's wild-caught seafood to Boston-area chefs.

Kim Marden prefers to work with small, chef-owned restaurants that work seasonally and are flexible about the fish they run on their menu. Seafood seasonality is something most chefs learn over time. "The longer a chef has been in business, they learn what not to put on the menu at certain times of year," Marden explains. When chefs work with a purveyor like Marden who can share tips and strategies, they can plan menus that change seasonally, feature local seafood, and keep their costs in line.

And even though Marden sells plenty of farmed fish and fish caught all over the world, he remains loyal to the hard-pressed fishermen of this region and passes that value on to his chefs. He tells them, "We're in Boston. You have to support the local guys because if we don't, they're not going to be there tomorrow."

Stuffed Rhode Island Squid

Serves 4 as a first course or light supper

1 lb. cleaned squid (about 6 tubes plus tentacles)
4 tbsp. extra virgin olive oil
1 tbsp. garlic, finely chopped
1 tbsp. shallots, minced
1 tbsp. Lucques olives, finely chopped
1 tbsp. parsley, chopped
3/4 tsp. Aleppo pepper
juice and zest of half a lemon
kosher salt and freshly ground black pepper
1/2 c. onion, cut into 1/4-inch dice
1/2 c. celery, peeled and diced 1/4-inch
1 tsp. paprika
1/2 c. white wine
1 c. fresh or canned tomatoes, peeled, seeded, and chopped
1 tsp. capers

Chop the squid tentacles to make about 1 c. Heat 1 tbsp. olive oil with half of the garlic and the shallots in a small sauté pan over medium heat and cook for 2 minutes. Add the tentacles and olives; season with salt; cook 1 minute and remove from the heat. Cool. Add the parsley and 1/4 tsp. Aleppo pepper and stir to combine.

Fill the squid tubes with a spoonful of the tentacle filling. Secure with a toothpick. Place in a large bowl and toss in the lemon juice and zest and 1/4 tsp. salt.

Heat the remaining oil in a large sauté pan over medium-high heat. Add the onion and celery and cook 5 minutes. Season with salt and pepper. Add the rest of the garlic, paprika, and remaining Aleppo pepper and cook 3 minutes. Add the wine and tomatoes and cook 4 minutes. Add the stuffed squid, cover with parchment, reduce the heat to low, and simmer 30 minutes. Turn the squid and cook an additional 30 minutes. Transfer squid to a platter.

Add the capers to the pan and reduce the sauce over low heat until it thickens. Serve with boiled red bliss potatoes tossed with chopped parsley and drizzled with extra virgin olive oil.

Squid

There are hundreds of varieties of squid, from creatures no bigger than your finger to those that do battle with sharks and Captain Nemo's submarine. If you encounter one on your dinner plate, it's typically *loligo pealei*, longfin squid, and odds are it came off of a Rhode Island fishing boat.

Loligo are found from Florida to Newfoundland and can be caught any time of the year, but they're notoriously unpredictable: you have to know where to find them. Rhode Island commercial fishermen are very good at this. The Ocean State fleet accounts for most of the 15 million pounds or more of loligo squid landed each year.

Once the fishermen have taken care of the difficult part, cooking squid is easy. It can be battered and fried, sautéed, blanched and served cold, simmered in sauce, or stuffed, filling the long, tubular body with a mixture of chopped tentacles, sautéed aromatics, and croutons.

Winter Squash and Mushroom Tart with Phyllo Crust

Makes 4 entrée servings

4 tbsp. olive oil

1 large white onion, sliced into 1/4-inch-thick rings (2 c.)

1 tbsp. red wine vinegar

kosher salt and freshly ground black pepper

2 tbsp. fresh flat-leaf parsley, chopped

1/2 lb. mushrooms, cut into 1/4-inch slices

1 tbsp. fresh ginger, minced

1 tsp. garlic, minced

2 tbsp. shallots, minced

1/2 c. Marsala wine

1 tsp. fresh thyme, chopped

1 tbsp. unsalted butter

12 oz. orange squash, peeled and sliced into 1/4-inch slices

4 oz. grated Gruyere cheese (about 1/2 c.)

4 sheets phyllo dough

Preheat oven to 400 degrees. Heat 1 tbsp. oil in a medium-sized sauté pan over medium heat. Add the onions, season with salt and pepper, and cook, stirring occasionally, until translucent (3–5 minutes). Reduce the heat to low and continue cooking, stirring occasionally, until the onions are golden, caramelized, and sweet (30–40 minutes). Add the vinegar and cook 1 minute. Cool. Season to taste with salt and pepper. Add the parsley.

Heat 1 tbsp. oil in a large sauté pan over medium heat. Add the mushrooms, season with salt and pepper, and cook until they are tender and their juices have evaporated (about 8 minutes). Transfer them to a plate. Add 1 tbsp. oil to the pan with the garlic and shallots. Cook 2 minutes. Return the mushrooms to the pan with the Marsala and cook until the Marsala has reduced to a glaze. Stir in the thyme; season to taste with salt and pepper. Cool.

In a small bowl, toss the squash with salt and pepper to coat evenly. Melt the butter in a 9-inch ovenproof sauté pan over medium heat. Off the heat, arrange squash slices in an overlapping fan in the bottom of the pan. Cover with the remaining slices. Spread the mushrooms over the squash; top with the cheese and then the onions.

Lay a phyllo sheet on a clean, dry, flat surface. Brush lightly with oil. Lay a second sheet on top and brush with oil. Repeat with the remaining two sheets, brushing the final sheet with oil. Cut the stack in half crosswise and set one stack on top of the other so the resulting stack has eight layers. Place the phyllo sheets on top of the mushrooms. Using scissors, cut off the corners so the phyllo fits over the vegetables in the pan.

Set the sauté pan over medium-high heat. When you hear the squash start to sizzle, move the pan to the floor of the oven and cook until the pastry is crisp and brown and the squash is tender and golden brown (30–40 minutes). Check to see if the squash is done by picking up the edge of the pastry.

Serve in wedges with a simple green salad.

Winter Squash & Mushroom Tart
with Phyllo Crust

winter

Winter in New England is a challenging season, for sure, especially as it drags into March, but it's hardly a barren landscape when it comes to local food, with farms extending the growing months, winter markets opening up, and some of the best seafood of the year coming into season. Great wintertime cooking also means working with a well-stocked pantry and an affinity for long, slow cooking processes, but when it's cold, icy, and dark, there are worse ways to spend your time than hovering over your stove.

Toro and Coppa

Chef Jamie Bissonnette
Round the Bend Farm

"Looking at a whole animal and not knowing what I'm going to do with it until I cut it up, it's kind of an adrenaline rush," says Jamie Bissonnette, the chef at Toro and Coppa and *FOOD & WINE*'s People's Choice for Best New Chef in 2011.

Whether it's calf's-brain ravioli or pig's-ear terrine, Bissonnette has been associated with offal and charcuterie since his first big job in Boston, running the kitchen at Eastern Standard Kitchen and Drinks. In his ten years of cooking in town, Bissonnette has spent most of them working with Ken Oringer, one of Boston's first high-profile chef-entrepreneurs. After working for Oringer briefly at his first restaurant, Clio, and then later at KO Prime, Bissonnette became a partner in Toro, and the two opened Coppa together in 2009.

Since early in his cooking career, the former vegan (he grew up in the straight-edge punk scene) says he's been fascinated by breaking down whole animals—and by the challenge of using every part. He's also learned on the job. "As a young cook, your chef's not going to give you a lobster to experiment with," he says. "Offal is cheaper."

"It's creative," says Bissonnette, of working nose-to-tail, "and it also makes me feel more responsible with the animal. It's like, that chicken didn't die so you could throw its feet in the trash."

The small plates format at Coppa was based on using whole animals. "You can only get so much offal out of one animal," he says. "But I can run specials and have enough for three or four plates, and it works." Coppa's esoteric twist on the corner enoteca has drawn crowds to its forty seats since opening in December 2009.

Bissonnette grew up in Hartford, Connecticut, in a household where he fended for himself in the kitchen. "My mother couldn't cook anything," he says. "Her signature dish we used to call 'gross-me-out.'" But Bissonnettte was inquisitive and loved to eat, so before long, he was cooking for himself and friends. He went to cooking school in Florida and finished when he was nineteen, landing in Boston in 2001.

As Bissonnette continues to work with whole animals, he's learned that "the more you know about where you're getting your animals, the better it's going to be." His pigs, goats, and lambs often come from his friend T Vieira at Round the Bend Farm. Produce comes from Matt Linehan from Sparrow Arc Farm in Maine.

Although Bissonnette works with local producers, he's quick to point out the limitations of being hyper focused on local food as a chef in New England. "If we didn't have the grilled corn year-round at Toro," he says, "I think we'd be closed." And Bissonnette doesn't make a statement about farm-to-table food. "I like to quote David Chang," he continues, "'I buy my food, I put it on a table, so I am farm to table.'"

But Bissonnette does work regularly with farms like Round the Bend, where Antone "T" Vieira and his wife, Elen, farm about fifty acres in South Dartmouth, in southeastern Massachusetts. Although Vieira's farming background is in produce, he says, "We got into raising

livestock because the land on this farm was pasture." The hilly, rocky terrain was better suited to animals than field crops, "so we chose the appropriate activity for the resources we had at hand."

They raise cattle, sheep, pigs, goats, and chickens. "It's a complete multi-species farm system," says Vieira. "You get all the animals together, and it's like having more tools in the toolbox for land management." With a main goal of self-sufficiency, the couple's business is based on selling the animals to chefs, mostly in the Boston area.

"Working with restaurants can be challenging," says Vieira, "but the best part is that you're engaging directly with the chefs, who are understanding and loyal." Vieira met a lot of his current customers when he worked as a grower and delivery driver for Eva Sommaripa, now his neighbor and a farmer well known to Boston chefs. He feels fortunate that those relationships dovetailed with the current craze for eating locally produced food.

"There's the security when you build up a friendship with someone who knows what you're about," says Vieira, "but there are challenges of full-bore going for locally raised meat." Raising animals the way Vieira believes they should be raised is expensive. Among other factors, a dwindling number of slaughterhouses available to process the meat often means a long drive for many farmers. As a result, says Vieira, "my stuff is priced in such a way that the chefs can't afford to bring it in all the time."

"It's very precarious, but we're all benefitted by the fact that it's chic to eat like this," he concludes. "But when people don't want to eat like this anymore, then what happens?"

Tripe with Matt's Tuscan Kale

Serves 6–8

The combination of tripe and a hearty green like kale is great. This is a good beginner dish for those who have never cooked tripe.

2 lbs. honeycomb tripe
3 c. dry white wine
1 c. salt
4 c. chicken stock
1 onion, roughly chopped
2 carrots, cut into chunks
2 celery sticks, cut into chunks
2 sachets of caraway, coriander, fennel seed, and mustard
   seed (about 1/2 tsp. of each for each sachet)
4 shallots, chopped
2 tbsp. olive oil
3 garlic cloves, sliced
1 Anaheim pepper, thinly sliced
1 Poland pepper, thinly sliced
1 red jalapeno, thinly sliced
1 fennel bulb, finely diced
1 c. applejack whiskey
1 10-oz. can plum peeled tomatoes, crushed (at the end of
   July/August, use 2 lbs. mixed heirloom tomatoes, diced)
3 lbs. Tuscan kale, stemmed, blanched, and shocked
Espelette pepper to taste (Espelette is a chili pepper native
   to Basque country in Europe, where it has replaced black
   pepper as a seasoning. It is warm and spicy but not too hot.)

Place tripe in a large pot and cover with water and 1 c. white wine; refrigerate and soak for 3–12 hours. Clean by scrubbing with the blunt side of a French knife, rinse, and cover again in a pot of cold water with 2 c. white wine and 1 c. salt. Bring to a simmer. Turn off immediately and strain.

Return the tripe to the pot, and cover the top of the tripe by 4 inches with chicken stock. Add onion, carrots, celery, and spice sachet. Bring to a boil, reduce to a low simmer, and cook for 5–6 hours with a tight-fitting lid. Cool the tripe overnight in its liquid.

For the stew: In a tall stockpot over medium heat, heat the olive oil and add the shallots. Cook until soft and translucent (about 10 minutes).

While cooking the shallots, bring the tripe back to a boil and strain, reserving the braising liquid. When the shallots are tender, add the garlic. Cook until garlic is translucent. Add all three peppers and the fennel. Cook over medium heat until tender (about 10–15 minutes). Add the strained tripe, sachet, and applejack and bring to a simmer. Add the tomatoes and the kale and continue simmering. Cook for 45 minutes, adding tripe braising liquid as needed. Thin to desired consistency with tripe liquid. Season to taste with salt and Espelette pepper.

Brussels Sprouts
with Horseradish

Serves 4–6 as a side

1 lb. Brussels sprouts
salt and fresh cracked pepper
1/4 c. extra virgin olive oil
3 tbsp. Prepared Horseradish (see recipe below)
1 tsp. Espelette pepper
1/4 c. Pecorino, grated (any salty aged sheep's milk cheese can be substituted)
1-inch piece fresh horseradish

Bring 2 gal. salted water to a boil. Get an ice bath ready. When the water comes to a boil, add the Brussels sprouts and cook until bright green and tender (about 5 minutes). Shock in the ice water and reserve.

Set an oven to 400 degrees. Season the Brussels sprouts with salt and pepper. Place them on a roasting tray. Roast them in the oven until hot and caramelized (15–20 minutes). Remove them from the tray and place in a mixing bowl. Season with the olive oil, prepared horseradish, Espelette, and Pecorino. Mix thoroughly. Taste and adjust seasoning. Serve in a bowl and grate the fresh horseradish over the top.

PREPARED HORSERADISH:

1 lb. horseradish, peeled and grated
2 c. white vinegar
2 c. water
1/8 c. salt
1 c. white sugar

Grate the peeled horseradish into a large bowl. In a separate medium-sized bowl, mix the vinegar, water, salt, and sugar. Stir until the sugar and salt are dissolved. Pour over the horseradish. Store in the refrigerator in a container with a tight-fitting lid for up to 2 weeks.

Brussels Sprouts

Brussels sprouts get a bad rap. The member of the wild cabbage family is high in compounds that give it a bitter taste, and when overcooked, it can emit a sulfurous odor that puts many people off. This is avoidable, and when cooked correctly, Brussels sprouts are a hearty, satisfying vegetable that store well and will keep green on your plate through the darkest days of the year.

Choose Brussels sprouts of uniform size—this will keep the cooking even and the texture consistent. The sprouts, which grow in little buds off of a long stalk (and when purchased from the farmers' market resemble a dangerous-looking green club), should be blanched in a big pot of salted boiling water and then immediately plunged into an ice bath. From there, they can be simply sautéed in butter, olive oil, or pork fat and served. Or they can be tossed with olive oil, seasoned, and roasted in a hot oven until they start to caramelize at the edges.

TW Food

Chef Tim Wiechmann
Drumlin Farm

"I'm kind of like a grumpy artist," says Chef Tim Wiechmann. The former professional guitar player once cooked to support his music career, but for more than a decade now, food has been his main creative outlet. If he's grumpy, you can't really tell by eating his food.

At TW Food, the twenty-eight-seat restaurant he runs with his wife, Bronwyn, Wiechmann sets high expectations for ingredient quality and makes most things by hand so he can have control over the process. The result is a very intimate, personal restaurant with sophisticated food and a dedicated clutch of regulars.

TW Food opened in 2007, when Wiechmann was thirty-three and fresh off of a series of stages in Europe where he apprenticed at renowned restaurants like Taillevent and Arpege in Paris. His food combines the refined sensibilities he learned in Europe with an earthy seasonality.

Before traveling to Europe to apprentice at those Michelin-starred restaurants, Wiechmann worked at well-known spots in Boston like Lumiere and Sel de la Terre. In 2001, he was the opening chef at Ten Tables in Jamaica Plain, where he and owner Krista Kranyak collaborated to bring the tiny neighborhood bistro to life. "We invented what it is today," says Wiechmann. "It was awesome. And when we did it, we weren't even really pros."

Even with years of experience working in and running kitchens, Wiechmann felt like a complete novice when he arrived in France. "Arpege and Taillevent—I got annihilated there, picked on," says the chef. "I had been humbled, but by the end, I was mercenary. I could go anywhere."

He decided to open his own place where he could have full creative control. At TW Food, some of Wiechmann's more esoteric creations have raised eyebrows, but the care and personality evident in every facet of the restaurant overwhelms any perceived missteps. It's fun to eat at a place where the chef is clearly running with his own creativity—if you have preconceived feelings about cumin ice cream with marinated vegetables, you might be surprised—a feeling that can be rare in restaurants these days.

Wiechmann takes extra steps to ensure his quality standards. "I always try and do things myself," he says. "I might face a learning curve, but that's the way it goes. Nobody who is good at anything was always good at it. If I try, I can usually figure things out myself." That includes butchering whole animals, mastering many European charcuterie techniques, milling his own flour for pasta and bread (both of which he makes from scratch), and cellaring his own root vegetables for winter storage.

"I'm in control of my own world here," says Wiechmann. "It's my menu, it's my name—I do what I want. Nobody's telling me I have do this, that, or the other thing. Which is priceless, man. That's why I do it."

All those crops in Wiechmann's root cellar were grown at Drumlin Farm, a few towns away from his home. Owned by conservation organization Mass Audubon, Drumlin Farm in Lincoln, Massachusetts, is known as a destination for families who want to spend the day outside, walking the wooded trails, petting the sheep, and learning about the lifecycles of sprouting plants.

Beyond that, the farm's CSA runs almost year-round by storing up to thirty-five thousand pounds of produce in its root cellar. The CSA is the farm's primary business model, says farm manager Matt Celona, who has run the farm for the past seven years. During the growing season of 2010, Drumlin started a restaurant sales program to help meet the farm's goal of selling everything that is harvested each week.

Restaurants can offer consistent business, points out Celona, "instead of harvesting and going to a weekday farmers' market where the sales are dependent on the weather and foot traffic. And we like working with restaurants because it's nice to see what they do with our food, to see the farm's name on the menu, and to get feedback from the chefs."

One way Drumlin stands out from other farms selling to restaurants is with season extension. Competition for restaurant business tightens in the summer, when more farms' products are available. But in the spring, and especially in the dead of winter, Drumlin's greenhouses and root cellar have a relative abundance of local food—kale and Brussels sprouts, squash, garlic and other root vegetables—for those on the lookout.

Drumlin's extended season has been great for the farm, attracting more visitors and more business, says Celona. But an extended winter means a shorter break for the farm crew. Even before it's time to start planting in the greenhouses, "maple sugar season is right around the corner."

Winter-Stored Parsnip Soup
with Local Wildflower Honey Cream

Serves 8

6–8 large "overwintered" parsnips (4 lbs. total)
8 c. (2 qt.) whole milk
8 tbsp. (1 stick) unsalted butter
3/4 c. local wildflower honey
1/2 c. heavy cream
salt and cracked black pepper

Peel the large parsnips and slice as thinly as possible. Place the slices in a medium-sized saucepan with the milk and bring to a boil. Lower to a simmer, stirring frequently. Cook until tender (about 25–30 minutes). Transfer to a blender and purée with butter, salt, pepper, and 1/2 c. of the honey. Pass through a very fine mesh strainer or chinois.

Whip the cream to soft peaks, incorporating the remaining 1/4 c. honey. Ladle the soup into bowls and serve with scoops of whipped cream.

Scallops

Bay scallops are jewels of the winter table. They are smaller and sweeter than their sea scallop cousins and are fleeting—their season is only open from November through March.

Scallops require little prep work (you may want to remove the tough adductor muscle the scallop uses to scoot around the ocean floor) and are fast and simple to prepare. They need nothing more than a little salt and pepper and a quick sear in a hot pan. They will develop a beautiful brown crust when seared for a couple of minutes. Don't overcook them because they turn rubbery fast.

Pan-Roasted Nantucket Bay Scallops

with Parsnips and Blood Orange

Pan-Roasted Nantucket Bay Scallops with Parsnips and Blood Orange

Serves 8 as an appetizer

1 lb. salted cod, soaked in water
3 c. whole milk
6 tbsp. unsalted butter
6 small fingerling potatoes (about 1 lb.)
6 large parsnips from root cellar, sliced
1 clove garlic
1 branch thyme
1 lb. Nantucket Bay scallops, cleaned
1 bunch Italian parsley
3 blood oranges, zest and segments
butter, olive oil, lemon, nutmeg to taste

Rinse the salted cod several times over the course of one hour.

In a small saucepan, bring 1 c. milk to a bare simmer.

In a medium-sized saucepan, boil the potatoes, peel while hot, and push through a food mill. Return to the saucepan and mash over high heat with a wooden spatula. Beat in 4 tbsp. butter. Finish with a splash of the hot milk and beat until smooth. Season with salt, pepper, and nutmeg. Cover and set aside.

Meanwhile, in another medium-sized saucepan, bring a second cup of milk to a bare simmer and add the garlic, thyme, and cod. Poach the cod for 8–10 minutes. Fold the cooked cod into the potatoes and set aside.

Set the oven to 500 degrees. Wash and peel the parsnips. Slice half of them thin.

In a medium-sized saucepan, bring the third cup of milk to a bare simmer, add the sliced parsnips, and poach until tender (about 12–15 minutes), adding in some blood orange zest. Purée with the poaching milk and 2 tbsp. butter, adjust seasoning with lemon, and reserve in a warm spot.

Slice the remaining parsnips into 1/4-inch coins and place on a sheet pan. Roast them, brushing with olive oil and salt occasionally, until tender (about 20 minutes).

In a large sauté pan, heat 2 tbsp. olive oil. Add the scallops and sear over high heat, basting with a little butter, about 2–3 minutes on each side.

Arrange an elegant plate with a dollop of cod mousseline, a stripe of parsnip purée, the roasted parsnips, the seared scallops, some Italian parsley leaves, and some blood orange segments.

606 Congress

Chef Rich Garcia
Blackbird Farm

Maine Lobster and Caviar Deviled Blackbird Farm Eggs

Serves 8–12 as an appetizer

12 large Blackbird Farm eggs
1/2 c. cooked Maine lobster, finely chopped
4 tbsp. homemade mayonnaise
1 tbsp. shallots, minced
1 tbsp. chives, minced
1 tsp. dry mustard powder
1/2 tsp. cayenne pepper
1/4 tsp. brown sugar
kosher salt to taste
juice of 1 lemon
American caviar for garnish

Place eggs in a 3-qt. pot with water to cover. Set the pot on the stove over high heat (uncovered). Let the eggs come to a boil and continue boiling until done; from the moment you put the eggs on the stove to removing them from the heat, it should be a total of about 12 minutes on a gas stove, 15 minutes on an electric stove. Cool the eggs by immediately placing them in an ice bath. Once the eggs are completely chilled, roll them on the counter with pressure from the palm of your hand to crack the shell. Carefully peel away the shell so as not to puncture the whites. Slice shelled eggs in half lengthwise, and separate the whites from the yolks. Set aside cleaned whites.

Finely grate the egg yolks into a mixing bowl (the finer you grate the egg yolks, the smoother the filling). Add the lobster, mayonnaise, shallots, chives, mustard, cayenne, brown sugar, salt, and lemon juice to the yolks. Combine until smooth. Spoon or pipe mixture into the reserved egg whites. Using the back of a small spoon, place a tiny amount of caviar on each egg. Serve immediately.

Tavolo

Chef Nuno Alves
Seafood Specialties

Growing up as the youngest of eleven children, Nuno Alves learned his way around the kitchen at an early age. His family emigrated from the Azores when Alves was five years old, and both parents maintained strong food traditions—keeping a garden and chickens in the backyard, and making most of their own staples like sausage, cheese, and wine. "If my mom doesn't have a fifty-pound bag of potatoes on hand, she's worried," says Alves.

Whether it was learning to stir rice pudding just right as a boy or learning the intricacies of regional Italian cooking during his eight years working for Jody Adams at Rialto, Alves has spent his life in the kitchen. From an early age, he learned the importance of good ingredients.

When his family first arrived in the United States, they settled in Inman Square, which at the time was filled with Portuguese immigrants. Alves visited the Chelsea Market to buy grapes for wine with his dad, and a truck market on Cardinal Medeiros Avenue sold meats, fish, and cheeses from farmers in Fall River and Taunton. Alves and his brothers and father often went cod fishing (and made their own salt cod), set and hauled lobster traps in Lynn, and caught tautog in South Boston.

The size of Alves's family meant his parents had to be extra-economical when they cooked. Making their own sausages and other cured meats was common. "Everyone's embracing head-to-tail cooking now," he says. "I used to eat this stuff on a regular basis—I didn't know it was fancy food."

Alves's first cooking job was at Cambridge City Hospital, where one of his sisters worked as a dietary supervisor. At first he was a dietary aide trainee, but he worked his way up to cooking on the line there. After two years, he applied for a prep job at Rialto. For the first year he worked there, Alves worked split shifts every day, walking between Rialto and the hospital.

He stayed at Rialto for eight years, working his way up to sous-chef. "Rialto just took it to the next level for me," he says. At first, he wasn't confident in the fine-dining restaurant kitchen. But he learned how to care for the ingredients, to treat each product separately, and to balance the flavors of New England ingredients with Jody Adams's style of regional Italian cuisine. He learned that "it was a different style of cooking than I grew up with, but with the same values at the base."

Alves's parents still live in his childhood home, and though all of the kids are grown, they continue to cook for crowds. His mother recently bought twenty pounds of kale and thirty pounds of cod through Alves. He shakes his head. "She says you never know who's going to stop by."

One of those people might be Chris Edelman, Alves's close friend and fish supplier. Edelman has a thing for uniforms. For his role as a seafood purveyor during the week, he wears green coveralls with his name sewn onto the chest. On Saturdays, "off goes the hard hat and the processing uniform, and on goes the tie and the fedora and the butcher coat," he says. Edleman wears the second getup to work the retail counter

at Wulf's, an old-school fish market just outside Boston he bought in 2010 to complement Seafood Specialties, the wholesale business he's owned since 2005.

The former chef attended culinary school in Vermont and spent sixteen years in the kitchen, including five as the owner of a small restaurant in Maine. "I knew I didn't want to cook for a living anymore," he says, but he wasn't sure what he wanted to do instead. A career counselor told Edelman he'd make a good fish guy, so Edelman went for it. "I wasn't interested in selling pallets of frozen crap," he says, so he searched until he found a company that matched his values. The owners also happened to be looking to sell.

Edelman went to work for Seafood Specialties in 2004 and bought it the following year. The company sells to chef-driven restaurants in Boston and around the country, and Edelman has built the business by providing the kind of attention to detail he knows chefs appreciate.

The business is labor-intensive. Edelman and his staff buy only what they need to fill their orders for the day, he says, and they scale, cut, skin, and bone out the fish all by hand, following individual specs for different orders. Taking orders, too, is a custom process. "Our product list is anything that's available," explains Edelman. "So it's a lot of nonstop telephone, Skype, text, email—what we see at the market and what chefs want to work with."

At Wulf's, the retail market, the attention to detail carries over. Edelman bought the third-generation family business with the agreement he'd keep the employees and the sensibilities of the business intact. "It's a family business," he says. He has plans for expanding Wulf's but intends to keep it "all about the fish."

Roasted Cod
with Littleneck Clams and Portuguese Chorizo

Roasted Cod with Littleneck Clams and Portuguese Chorizo

Serves 4

4 6-oz. cod fillets
3 tbsp. olive oil
12 littleneck clams
2 tbsp. shallot, minced
1 c. chorizo, diced
2 c. lobster broth
1 c. white wine
1 lb. red potatoes, cut into 1/2-inch dice and sautéed
1 bunch kale, stemmed, blanched, shocked, and roughly chopped
1 tsp. parsley, chopped
pinch fresh tarragon, chopped
salt and cracked black pepper

Set the oven to 350 degrees. In a large sauté pan over high heat, add the olive oil. When it shimmers, add the cod fillets. Cook for 5 minutes, or until you can see the flesh near the bottom starting to turn opaque. Flip it over, cook for 5 more minutes, and place the skillet in the oven for 6–7 minutes. Remove the cod from the pan. Set it on a platter and cover.

Place the same pan over medium heat. Add the clams, shallot, chorizo, lobster broth, and white wine. Bring to a simmer and cover pan until clams open up (about 5 minutes). Take clams out of the pan and set aside.

Add kale and potatoes to the pan and return to a simmer. Add cod, tarragon, and parsley. Return the clams to the pan and simmer all ingredients together for a minute or two.

To serve: Layer the potatoes in each of the bowls. Layer the kale over the potatoes, then place the cod on top of the kale. Place the clams around the cod and pour the lobster broth sauce around the cod.

Cod

A linchpin of early global trade, Atlantic cod is a legendary fish that's long been one of the most important food sources to come out of the ocean. But over time, it has been overfished, and *gadus morhua* is no longer a marine resource that communities depend on. More recently, strict measures have been put in place to limit the amount of cod that can be caught by commercial fishermen, easing pressure on the populations and allowing the females to reproduce before they are caught.

Despite (or maybe because of) the fishery's woes, cod remains a sought-after fish. Its dense, flaky meat is light but full of flavor, and it can be prepared in hundreds of ways, including salt-cured—a traditional preservation method still used by some cooks to achieve a specific flavor and texture with the fish.

Rich Lobster Cream Sauce

Yield: About 2 qt.

1/3 c. canola oil
2 carrots, diced
2 celery stalks, diced
4 leeks, diced
4 shallots, sliced thinly
4 cloves garlic, sliced
10 lobster bodies, roasted and crushed
1 c. brandy
3 c. white wine
4 c. canned tomatoes, put through a food mill
3 c. white wine
water
1 bunch parsley stems
1 bunch basil stems
1 c. heavy cream

Heat the canola oil in a large stockpot over medium heat. Add the carrots, celery, leeks, shallots, and garlic, and cook, stirring frequently, until tender and translucent (about 15 minutes). Add the lobster bodies and cook, stirring frequently, for about 10–12 minutes. Add the brandy, white wine, and tomatoes. Bring to a boil, reduce to a high simmer, and cook until liquid is reduced and thickened (about 20 minutes). Add the herb stems. Add water until it just covers the lobster bodies. Bring to a boil, reduce heat, and simmer for 45 minutes, or until reduced by half. Strain and return broth to the pot. Add heavy cream and simmer until the liquid is reduced by 25 percent. Strain and cool. Serve over roasted cod filets and freeze remaining sauce for future use.

In the kitchen with his father, Chef Nuno Alves continues the family's cooking traditions.

Bondir

Chef Jason Bond

Pete and Jen's Backyard Birds and Farmyard

At his first restaurant job at a burger joint by the highway in Manhattan, Kansas, Jason Bond got in trouble for trying to make things prettier. A music student at Kansas State, Bond grew up around avid home cooks—both grandmothers kept gardens, and "they were all about preserving things and putting things up," says Bond.

Once he realized that cooking was a viable career option, Bond began to study—reading and trying out recipes whenever he could. By graduation, he was rarely without a cookbook under his arm, he says, and he has made a careful study of the profession ever since. In 2010, he opened his first restaurant, Bondir, a twenty-eight-seat spot with a menu that changes daily and showcases his thoughtful, precise cooking style. "When I think about the style of the menu or the message I try to get across," he explains, "it's imagining the ideal meal and trying to get as close to that as possible."

Bond's kitchen also runs on two tracks: reacting to what's coming in from his network of local and international producers every day, and planning the pantry of preserved foods that gird his menus. And he uses every part of the ingredients. For example, Bond explains, when bronze fennel is in season, they might braise or shave the fresh bulb, "but we use every piece of it year-round. We make fennel pollen to last the year, fennel seeds we dry for the year, and so on."

After college, Bond moved to Vermont to attend culinary school, but he was restless in the classroom. After a couple of months, he left and embarked on a self-styled apprenticeship. "The next few years I just spent harassing chefs I wanted to learn from," he says. Bond worked for renowned bakers and restaurant owners, trying to soak up as much cooking technique as possible, as well as learning how successful restaurateurs seemed to have control of the big picture.

A job at Formaggio Kitchen, a specialty foods store in Cambridge with a huge selection of cheeses and other products from all over the world, "was my true culinary school," says Bond. "You can taste more products than you ever could in a restaurant, and you get a really intimate idea of these ingredients and how they change season to season."

Bond stayed at Formaggio for two years, followed by a string of moves that filled holes in his knowledge: working as a general manager, working in a hotel, opening and running restaurants as executive chef in both the city and the country. By the time he found the little spot that is now Bondir, he felt prepared to own his own place. "You're never going to know everything," he says. "But at some point you just have to take the leap and do it."

Over the years, Bond has made connections with many area producers, including Pete Lowy and Jen Hashley, who have raised animals specifically for him on their Concord farm.

When Lowy and Hashley opened up ordering for their 2011 chickens, the Concord farmers sold out in hours. Demand for their pasture-raised birds far outpaces supply, even as the couple's farm

has expanded over the past few years. If you've tasted the chicken, you'd be tempted to get in line too. The farmers raise a tasty bird.

Hashley and Lowy, former Peace Corps volunteers, both have other full-time jobs in agriculture: Lowy works as the farm manager at Verrill Farm, next door, and Hashley is the director of the New Entry Sustainable Farming Project, which trains new immigrants to become farmers. They also raise pigs, rabbits, and produce on their land, which they lease from Lowy's boss, Steve Verrill.

The two got into raising livestock because they wanted to produce their own food, says Hashley, who spent years as a vegetarian because she opposed factory farming. "I had no interest in supporting that system," she continues. "I really wanted to know exactly where my food was coming from." The best bet, thought she and Lowy, was to grow and raise it themselves.

What started with a couple of laying hens for eggs in 2003 has grown over time—in 2011 Lowy and Hashley were up to six hundred chickens. They emphasize pasture management in their livestock operations, rotating the animals through different fields at different times and making sure the grass gets the nutrients and treatment it needs to thrive.

In the process of building up their farm, Hashley and Lowy have also built quite a community of parents and children, city slickers, chefs, and others in search of good, local food. "The support and interest has been amazing," says Hashley. "It's great to be able to be that connection to people's food."

Jason's Blood Sausage (From Isabell Wiesner)

Yield: About 10–12 pounds of sausage

A pig's head, fat, blood, and skin can be ordered in advance from a butcher or local pig farm. The skin can be from the head or, even better, from the trotters or back fat. You need a kitchen scale and an extra-large stockpot, and the sausages may be frozen after they are simmered and cooled.

MEAT AND BROTH:

  1 pig's head (about 12 lbs.)
  5 lbs. pork belly
  3 onions, halved
  10 whole cloves
  salt

Place the head, belly, onions, and cloves in a large stockpot. Cover with cold water. Season generously with salt. Bring the liquid to a boil. Reduce the heat and simmer for 8 hours or until the meat on the head is tender and beginning to separate from the bone. Remove the head and belly from the liquid and transfer to a metal rack placed on a rimmed baking sheet. Allow the meat to cool slightly. Wearing gloves, separate the meat from the skin and the bones and discard the bones.

Meanwhile, simmer the broth for an additional hour. Remove and discard the onions. Save the broth for simmering the sausages.

SAUSAGE:

  7 oz. large-diameter beef casing (or synthetic casing of similar
    wide diameter)
  2 tsp. pork fat
  2 onions, diced
  6.6 lbs. picked pork meat and fat, in large pieces
  2.2 lbs. pork skin, finely diced or ground
  1 lb. rice, cooked and cooled
  1 lb. broth
  2 lbs. pig's blood
  5 oz. sea salt
  0.17 oz. (about 1 tsp.) curing salt #1
  0.17 oz. (about 1 tsp.) ground black pepper
  0.52 oz. (about 3 tsp.) ground allspice
  0.17 oz. (about 1 tsp.) ground nutmeg
  0.35 oz. (about 2 tsp.) dried marjoram
  0.35 oz. (about 2 tsp.) dried basil

Rinse and soak beef casing for at least 30 minutes. Wrap the end of the casing around the faucet and run water through the entire portion. Set aside.

In a skillet, heat 2 tsp. pork fat over medium heat. Add onions and cook for 5 minutes or until tender. Transfer to a plate to cool.
In a very large bowl, combine all of the ingredients except the casing. Gently mix to combine. Using a ladle or a sausage stuffer, fill the sausage casing with the filling, tying off as necessary.

Heat the remaining broth to 160 degrees. Poach the links for 20 minutes (or 10 minutes per inch of diameter). Chill. Slice and discard casing. Serve chilled with toast and mustard fruits.

Grilled and Marinated Tamworth Pork Heart Salad

Serves 4

At Bondir, we have several heritage breed pigs raised for us each year. They are raised on pasture and wooded areas and given organic feed, and we know them from piglet to porchetta. Last year, we had a group of Tamworth and Large Black pigs, one dozen each, and two remarkable Mangalitsa hogs, the only two on the East Coast being raised by a restaurant. This recipe is for a salad we serve with pork liver mousse.

1 fresh pork heart

2 tbsp. Pommery vinegar, methode d'Orleans

1/2 c. extra virgin olive oil

sel gris, black pepper from a mill

handful of mixed garden herbs (flowering thyme, lemon thyme, calamint, cicely, bronze fennel, etc.)

2 c. arugula

Prepare a hot grill. Trim all fat and connective tissue from the heart and butterfly evenly. Season the heart on both sides with salt and pepper. Place on the grill and place a grill weight or an iron skillet with a can in it to weigh down the heart. Mark well on the first side, then flip and mark lightly on the second side. The heart should still be raw to rare after cooking on both sides. It will carry over to between rare and medium rare.

From the grill, place in a nonreactive container and add the vinegar, the olive oil, the herbs, and another bit of salt and pepper. Allow to cool in this marinade for several hours, up to one day, before serving.

To serve: Slice the heart very thinly and toss with arugula. Dress with the marinade and serve as a light salad course or as a rose-colored and brightly flavored accompaniment to a charcuterie platter.

offal

Literally derived from the words "off-fall," according to the *Oxford Companion to Food*, offal is the term used for what's left of a carcass after it's been butchered—heart, lungs, brain, kidneys, feet, and so forth—and here in the United States, we don't eat much of it.

But among thrifty and creative cooks (at home and in restaurants), popularity of these so-called variety meats is on the rise. Whether it's due to more adventurousness among cooks and eaters or a deeper understanding of using ingredients responsibly, offal is coming into its own. For people who haven't eaten many organ meats, mild ones like liver and hearts of smaller animals provide a good point of entry.

Tastings Wine Bar and Bistro

Chef Matt Maue

Brambly Farms

"I guess I'm kind of earthy-crunchy," says Chef Matt Maue, a former vegetarian who takes the commuter rail to work outside of Boston and rides his bike the twenty-six miles home to his Bay Village neighborhood.

As the executive chef at Tastings Wine Bar and Bistro in Foxborough, a forty-minute drive southwest from Boston, Maue's inner tree-hugger, paired with his proximity to area farms, helps define his cooking style. Maue's ingredients are mostly local and seasonal, and he works with heirloom veggie varieties with ties to the region. The chef buys whole pigs and poultry and lesser-known cuts and parts of beef from two nearby livestock producers. "Growing up, I thought that all meat came from factories," he says. "It's important for me to support people who are doing the right thing."

To challenge his skills and keep his food costs down, he integrates all of the animal parts into his menus. Located next to Gillette Stadium, where the Patriots play football, Tastings sells tons of burgers. Surprisingly, beef heart Bolognese and beef tongue tacos are two top sellers. "I always try and keep offal on the menu," says Maue. "At first I didn't think it would sell. But I really think people's minds are opening and their palates are expanding."

Maue's been working in restaurants since he started washing dishes at a joint in his hometown of Buffalo, New York, at age fifteen. "I looked up to the chef," he says. "I thought, *that's something I could do.*" Maue worked his way up to cooking at a number of Buffalo restaurants, including a gastro-pub ("before there were gastro-pubs," he mentions), a restaurant inside an art gallery, and a Vietnamese restaurant where, as the sous-chef, he learned how to place orders for food in Vietnamese.

But Maue soon maxed out on the city's restaurant scene. In terms of his career, he says, "I didn't feel like I could go anywhere," so he packed his bags and headed to Atlanta. While there, he met friend Rich Garcia, with whom he moved to the Virgin Islands to open a sushi restaurant. He worked in a string of kitchens in the Virgin Islands and jumped at the chance to return to the Northeast, again to open a restaurant—Tastings—with Garcia. "When you're working in the Islands, you don't get good ingredients," he explains. "I wanted to get back to that."

In Foxborough, turning great ingredients into approachable food has been Maue's focus. "I'm definitely growing, maturing, in a sense," says the chef, who turned thirty in 2011. "I've always been really thrilled with the arts aspect of cooking, experimented with molecular gastronomy and so on. But as I'm getting older, my palate is getting simpler, so I see that you don't need all those sauces and stuff. You just need simple food, cooked properly." And maybe a shorter bicycle commute.

But as it stands in Foxborough, he's close to one of his favorite farmers, Ted O'Hart of Brambly Farms in Norfolk.

O'Hart is optimistic. "We stopped losing money farming two years ago," he says. Not bad for a farming enterprise that started as a project hatching chicks for one of his daughters' classes only a few years before that. O'Hart sells to a handful of Boston-area chefs now, but with plans to increase sales of his heritage pigs—as well as turkeys, rabbits, eggs, and geese—to chefs in Boston and hopefully New York, O'Hart estimates the farm will turn a profit in the next year or two.

With a limited amount of land on the Norfolk farm, O'Hart knew he couldn't keep too many animals. "So we thought we might as well keep special ones," he says. O'Hart did some research and chose three different pig breeds that would grow well on pasture and forage: Tamworth, Gloucester Old Spot, and Large Black. He keeps a number of these heritage breeds on the farm and crosses them with Berkshire ("the ultimate pig," says O'Hart), which means "we wind up with some pretty special animals."

The special pigs require a special customer, which is why he's pursued the high-end restaurant market. Unlike retail customers, chefs usually buy the whole animal—head, feet, and sometimes blood included. For chefs, it means more raw materials to turn into menu items. For O'Hart, it means fewer trips to the slaughterhouse and less time spent educating consumers about using (and buying) lesser-known cuts.

Brambly Farms may have started as a modest school project, but O'Hart is no hobbyist. The fifth-generation farmer grew up on an intensive livestock farm with twenty thousand broiler chickens, one hundred sows, and sixty milking cows in his native Ireland, and he farmed in Holland, France, and Australia before moving to the United States and eventually starting Brambly. "I'm not too good at growing vegetables," he admits, "but I do love the livestock."

Fried Brambly Farms Headcheese

Serves 8

1 pig's head
1 Spanish onion
6 sprigs thyme
2 bay leaves
1 bunch parsley stems
4 pig trotters
salt and pepper to taste
1 tsp. grated nutmeg

BREADING:
4 eggs
2 c. flour
4 c. panko breadcrumbs
salt and pepper to taste
1 c. vegetable oil

In a large stockpot, combine the pig's head, onion, thyme, bay leaves, parsley, and trotters, and add enough water to cover the head by an inch or two. Place on the stovetop on low heat and cook for 7–8 hours or until the meat is falling off the bone. Cool.

Center a large cutting board on a sheet pan. When the liquid is cool, wearing gloves, pull the head out off the liquid and place on the cutting board. Pick off all the meat, placing it in a bowl or plastic container. Discard the skin, bones, and brain.

Meanwhile, strain the liquid through a fine mesh sieve. Pick out the meat from the trotters and add to the bowl with the meat from the head. Discard the skin, bones, onions, and herbs. Place half of the liquid back into the stockpot, bring to a boil, reduce heat to medium, and cook until the liquid is reduced by half. If you like, reserve the remaining liquid for another use, such as soup or stew. Transfer to a storage container and place in the fridge or freezer. Discard what you're not using.

After all the meat is pulled from the bone, drizzle about half a cup of broth onto the meat to act as a gelling agent. You do not want it to be to wet. Season liberally with salt, pepper, and nutmeg.

Place half of the meat on an 18-inch-long sheet of plastic wrap and roll into a long, tight cylinder. Tie each end with twine. Repeat with the remaining meat and place in the refrigerator for 24 hours, turning occasionally to maintain the cylindrical shape.

To bread the headcheese: Beat the eggs in one bowl; place flour and panko in two separate bowls. Season the flour and panko with salt and pepper. Slice the headcheese into eight 1/2-inch slices. Dip each piece in egg first, followed by flour, then panko.

In a large, heavy-bottomed skillet, heat about a cup of vegetable oil over medium heat. When oil is shimmering, add the slices of headcheese, four at a time, and fry over medium heat. Cook until golden brown, about 2 minutes on each side. Line a plate with paper towels and place the headcheese there to drain off excess oil.

Arrange two pieces of head cheese on each plate and serve with a green salad with mustard vinaigrette.

* Note: There will be plenty of headcheese left over; it can be served sliced, cool or at room temperature, alone or as part of a charcuterie plate—it does not have to be fried.

Parsnip Gnocchi
with Mixed Mushrooms

Serves 4

1 lb. parsnips, peeled (about 4–6 medium parsnips)

1 1/2 c. flour, sifted

1/4 c. aged cow's milk cheese, grated (Blythedale Grana)

1 tsp. salt

1/2 c. plus 1 tsp. extra virgin olive oil

2 tbsp. fresh garlic, chopped

2 c. mixed fresh mushrooms (cremini and oyster mushrooms
  work fine if you can't find wild mushrooms)

salt and pepper to taste

1 bunch Swiss chard, ribs and stems removed, chopped

splash dry white wine

2 tsp. preserved lemon, rinsed and julienned

1 1/2 tbsp. fresh thyme leaves, chopped

1 1/2 tbsp. fresh parsley, chopped

1/4 c. Grana, grated

Add parsnips to a large pot of cold salted water and bring to a boil. Cook the parsnips until tender (about 10–15 minutes). Drain and set aside. Add to a food processer and purée while still warm.

In a large mixing bowl, combine the parsnips and the flour. Mix thoroughly. Mix in the cheese. Season with salt and mix well. Wrap the dough up in plastic wrap and allow the dough to rest for at least 1 hour. (The dough can rest for 48 hours until you are ready to use it.)

On a lightly floured surface, roll the gnocchi mixture into a thick, snake-like shape (about 1 inch diameter). Cut into small 3/4-inch pieces. Roll each piece into an oval shape. Set aside until ready to cook. Bring a large pot of salted water to a boil. Drop in the gnocchi until they begin to float. Pull from the water with a small strainer, let the water drain off, and set aside.

Heat the olive oil in a large sauté pan over medium heat. When it is hot and shimmering, add the garlic and mushrooms. Cook, stirring occasionally, for about 10 minutes, until the mushrooms have softened. Season with salt and pepper. Add the gnocchi and toss to combine. Cook, stirring for 2–3 minutes, then reduce the heat to low.

In a separate medium-sized sauté pan over medium heat, add 1 tsp. olive oil and the chard. Toss the chard with the oil and cook until chard is thoroughly wilted (about 3–4 minutes). Add the wilted chard to the pan with the gnocchi and toss to combine. Add the wine and simmer for 3–4 minutes until most of the wine has evaporated. Add lemon, thyme, and parsley to the pan. Check seasoning.

To serve: Arrange the gnocchi in four shallow bowls. Top with mushroom and chard mix. Shave the Grana over the pasta and serve.

Parsnips

Compared to its close relative the carrot, the parsnip pales in color only. The tapered tubers are starchier than carrots, and when the temperatures drop, the starch converts to sugar, giving spring-dug parsnips an extra layer of sweetness in addition to its peppery, nutty flavor.

Parsnips are delicious roasted or simmered in milk and puréed. They can be added to potato purée to punch up the flavor and are a natural complement to their relative, the carrot. Try both roasted with cumin and nutmeg for an easy and satisfying winter side dish.

The Gallows

Chef Seth Morrison

Snappy Lobster

"I want people to come here and know where they are when they look at the menu," says Seth Morrison, executive chef at the Gallows, the restaurant and bar he runs with proprietor Rebecca Roth.

The Gallows opened in June 2010 in Boston's South End. In a neighborhood cluttered with restaurants, the Gallows stands out for its genuine hospitality, its seasonal, playful food, and its design: rustic-chic with more than a hint of goth.

Morrison describes his sensibilities as "right here, right now"—food that's grounded in geography and the seasons. You taste early spring in a farmer's platter with pickled ramps, radishes, and stinging nettle frittata; early fall in a fried green tomato, pulled pork, and pic-calilli entrée—a pork dish that will be completely different four weeks later. There are way more than four seasons at play in Morrison's interpretation of New England food.

Morrison grew up in the suburbs west of Boston. His dad was a teacher, and every summer, the family traveled. "We camped up and down the East Coast, and during those trips I really got a sense of landscape and seasons and regional cultures," says Morrison. "I remember visiting Acadia National Park in Maine and eating wild Maine blueberries and lobster and corn and knowing we were doing something special to that time and place."

Like many cooks of his time, Morrison's education in food started on TV, watching a tall lady with a funny voice butcher slippery fish and flip giant pancakes on PBS. Julia Child and the Frugal Gourmet gave him the cooking bug, he says. As a grade-schooler, Seth would attempt elaborate meals for his family, including a Chinese banquet that he couldn't stay awake to eat one New Year's Eve. "I always understood cooking," he explains. "It was like a science experiment."

After an initial stab at college, Morrison began his first restaurant job scrubbing moldy refrigerators at John Harvard's Brewpub, followed by a return to and graduation from college and then a management position helping John Harvard's expand regionally. Leaving John Harvard's to get back into cooking, he landed at the East Coast Grill, where he learned about local and seasonal food and cooking and absorbed some of chef and owner Chris Schlesinger's rugged, playful style.

East Coast Grill was followed by a gig running a restaurant in Vieques, Puerto Rico, where, despite the guava tree in the backyard, Morrison missed New England's seasons and flavors. He headed home after two years and took a job running the kitchen at the now-closed Perdix, a small South End spot that allowed him to test his culinary voice.

Morrison also met business partner Rebecca Roth at Perdix—she took her first restaurant job cooking on the line there—and the two made plans to open the Biltmore together in 2006. Located just outside Boston, the Biltmore raised the bar for pub food in Boston

and gave Morrison and Roth a chance to polish their style and systems before opening the Gallows in one of the city's most competitive neighborhoods for dining.

At the Gallows, the menu covers the range of influences that make up this region's contemporary cuisine—from New England boiled dinner to altajena, a Portuguese stew of smoky pulled pork, clams, and potatoes—all made with ingredients sourced from a circle of friends, farmers, and purveyors Morrison has worked with over the years, including Adam Fuller of Snappy Lobster.

In 2008, before Fuller was driving a refrigerated truck full of lobsters around Boston, the Massachusetts native and trained chef had moved with his wife to her hometown of Derby, Kansas, a Wichita suburb. The couple lasted about seven months before returning to the East Coast. The landlocked location wasn't working for Fuller, who grew up on the North River in Norwell, south of Boston. "I just missed the water," he says.

Fuller's business, Snappy Lobster, which he runs with partner and lobsterman Larry Trowbridge, specializes in lobster caught off the coast of Scituate, along with whelks, Jonah crab, and other assorted species their network of fishermen bring in. Their customer base—higher-end restaurants in Boston—comes mostly from Fuller's relationships created during his days as a fine dining chef in the city.

Fuller and Trowbridge met at a dinner party soon after Fuller returned from Kansas in 2008, a very bad year for lobster prices. Trowbridge had been selling his catch at various farmers' markets, hoping the direct marketing would allow him to get a higher price per pound for his product.

Trowbridge had a product, and Fuller knew there was a huge void in the marketplace for fresh, locally caught lobster, so the two teamed up. They loaded Trowbridge's refrigerated truck full of a thousand pounds of lobster and started knocking on restaurants' doors, telling the chefs, "This is what a Massachusetts lobster looks like."

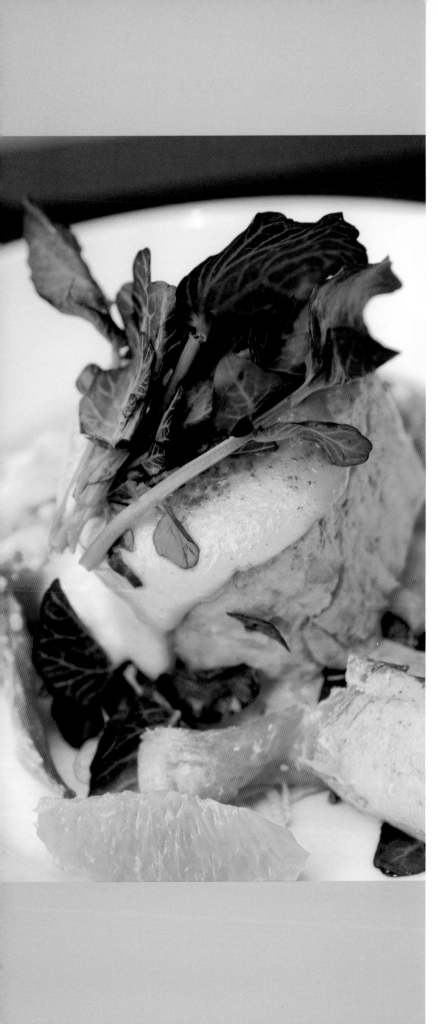

Lobster Sausage with Winter Salad

Serves 6

This recipe seems complex when you read through it for the first time, but it is really a series of relatively simple steps. The first step is to cook the lobster and remove the meat from the bodies (called shucking). This can be done by your fishmonger (ask to bring home the lobster bodies for stock), or you can look up directions for shucking a lobster online or in many seafood cookbooks. The sausage can be made ahead and refrigerated for a few days before assembling the entire dish.

STOCK:

- 1 c. vegetable oil
- 6 lobster bodies, rinsed, head sac removed
- 1 tsp. fennel
- 1 tsp. whole coriander
- 1/2 tsp. white pepper
- pinch saffron
- 2 bay leaves
- 2 tbsp. tomato paste
- 1 large carrot, peeled and chopped
- 1 medium yellow onion, peeled and chopped
- 3 celery stalks, chopped
- stalks of 2 medium fennel bulbs, chopped
- 3 qt. water (approximately)

In a large, heavy-bottomed pot over medium heat, heat 1 c. vegetable oil. Add the lobster bodies and toast them, stirring until they turn a deep reddish brown and the oil turns red (about 30 minutes). Add the fennel, coriander, white pepper, saffron, and bay leaves. Toast the seasonings, stirring, for 10 minutes until they are aromatic. Add the tomato paste and cook for 2 minutes, stirring regularly. Add the carrot, onion, celery, and fennel and cook, stirring, for 5 minutes. Add water to just cover the lobster and vegetables (about 3 quarts).

Bring to a boil and reduce heat to medium. Simmer for 45 minutes, skimming any foam that rises to the top. Strain and cool completely in the refrigerator. Once the liquid is completely cool, skim the oil off of the top and reserve.

SAUSAGE:
  1/2 lb. fresh Maine shrimp, peeled
  5 eggs, separated
  1/8 tsp. white pepper
  1/4 tsp. salt
  1/4 c. heavy cream
  1 lb. lobster meat, picked (meat from 6 1–1 1/4-lb. lobsters)
  1 tsp. fresh chives, chopped
  1 tbsp. fresh parsley, chopped
  1 tsp. fresh tarragon, chopped
  1 tbsp. unsalted butter (for greasing the foil)

In a food processor, combine shrimp and egg whites and process until smooth. Add the white pepper and salt. With the processor running, add the cream in a thin stream.

Transfer to a large mixing bowl and fold in the chopped lobster meat. Fold in the chives, parsley, and tarragon. Place the bowl in the refrigerator.

Lay out two pieces of aluminum foil, 18 inches long. Spray or grease with room-temperature unsalted butter. Layer plastic wrap of the same size over the greased foil. Working horizontally, arrange half of the mix into a 9-inch-long log (leaving an inch or so of space at either end), between 1 1/2–2 inches in diameter, an inch from the bottom of the foil. Fold the foil up and over the lobster mix to create a cylinder of foil around the sausage mix. Turn the foil four times, crimping the ends as you go to tighten up the cylinder. After the fourth turn, pinch the ends—one counter-clockwise, one clockwise to seal the cylinder. The tube will expand as you close the ends. This is normal.

Repeat the entire process with the second half of the lobster mix. Place the two foil-wrapped cylinders of lobster sausage in the refrigerator for at least an hour or up to 2 days.

To cook the sausage: Bring the stock to a bare simmer in a wide, deep saucepan. Add the foil-wrapped tubes of sausage and poach, maintaining the simmer (do not bring to a boil) for 35 minutes. The sausage will puff up during cooking. Remove from the liquid and cool completely.

When cool, unwrap the sausage from the foil. Have two 18-inch long sheets of plastic wrap ready. Lay the sausage down toward the end of the plastic wrap and roll tightly, pinching the ends counter-clockwise on one end, clockwise on the other. Refrigerate until ready to assemble the salad.

SALAD:
  reserved egg yolks from above
  1 tbsp. Dijon mustard
  2 tbsp. lemon juice
  2 garlic cloves
  salt and pepper to taste
  vegetable oil (about 1 c.)
  2 fennel bulbs, thinly sliced
  2 blood oranges, peeled and segmented, juice reserved
  1 bunch watercress, trimmed
  2 tbsp. olive oil
  2 tbsp. unsalted butter
  chives

TO ASSEMBLE:
Make the aioli: In a food processor, add the reserved egg yolks, Dijon, lemon juice, garlic, and salt and pepper to taste. Pulse everything in the food processor. Add enough vegetable oil to the reserved lobster oil to bring the yield to 2 c. Add the oil with the processor running. Adjust seasoning and reserve.

Place the fennel slices, oranges, and watercress in a bowl. Add the olive oil, salt, and pepper and mix to combine.

Remove the sausage from the refrigerator. With the plastic wrap still on, cut the sausage into six disks about 1 inch thick (there will be leftover sausage—reserve for a different use). Remove the plastic wrap. In a large nonstick sauté pan, heat 2 tbsp. butter over medium heat. Crisp the sausages on one side, cook for 3–4 minutes. Preheat the broiler. Flip the sausages, add a heaping teaspoon of aioli onto each sausage disk, and heat under the broiler until browned (2–3 minutes).

Assemble the salad onto six plates, and finish each salad with one disk of sausage, aioli side up. Garnish with snipped chives.

Corned Beef Short Rib Boiled Dinner

Serves 6

1 c. sugar
3–4 c. salt
1 tbsp. mustard seeds
1 tbsp. peppercorn
1 tbsp. fennel seeds
1 tbsp. coriander
5 allspice berries
5 cloves
4 bay leaves
2 tsp. chili flakes
6 beef shortribs (3/4–1 lb. each)
3 Yukon Gold potatoes, peeled and cut into 2-inch chunks
3 large carrots, peeled and cut into 2-inch chunks
3 parsnips, cut into 2-inch chunks
2 large turnips, peeled and cut into 2-inch chunks
1 head green cabbage, cut into quarters, core intact
1/4 c. whole grain mustard
1/4 c. horseradish

Combine the sugar, salt, mustard seeds, peppercorn, fennel seeds, coriander, allspice, and cloves into a large stockpot with 3 qt. water. The water should taste like very salty seawater. Bring to a boil. Turn off, and cool the brine completely, overnight.

Place the short ribs in a large mixing bowl or plastic container. Pour the brine over the ribs to cover them. Place a plate that is slightly smaller than the diameter of the bowl on top of the ribs and weigh it down to keep the ribs submerged in the brine (a can or two of food would work here). Brine the short ribs in the fridge for 4 days. Remove the ribs from the brine and rinse. Cover with water and soak for 12 hours. Drain.

Place the ribs in a large 3-qt. pot and cover with water. Bring to a boil. Remove the ribs, discard the water and rinse the pan, and return the ribs to the pot. Cover with water, bring to a boil, add the bay leaves and chili flakes, and reduce heat to a simmer. Simmer for 2 1/2 to 3 hours until the ribs are easily pierced with a fork. After 2 hours, add the potatoes, carrots, parsnips, turnips, and cabbage. Simmer until the vegetables are tender (about 20 minutes).

To serve: Divide the vegetables between six bowls. Add one short rib and 1/4 c. broth per bowl. In a medium-sized mixing bowl, add 1/4 c. whole grain mustard, 1/4 c. horseradish, and 1/4 c. broth and whisk together. Drizzle over each bowl of boiled dinner or serve on the side.

Proprietor of the Gallows, Rebecca Roth, and Chef Seth Morrison.

Lobster

As iconic as the codfish is to the identity of coastal Massachusetts (and all of New England), lobster enjoys association with corn, tomatoes, and long summer days—even though some lobstermen haul their traps practically year-round. To preserve their freshness, lobsters are almost always sold live, though in the mid-1800s, according to food historian Sandra Oliver, lobster canning was a growth industry in coastal New England.

Today, the lobster industry in Massachusetts is robust, but it faces steep competition from Canadian lobster that gets shipped south. And although the sweet, buttery-tasting meat works well in any number of preparations—baked and stuffed, bisque or fish stew, chilled and added to salad—it is perhaps at its best served "in the rough" (in its shell), with melted butter, by the shore.

Restaurant Directory

606 Congress
606 Congress Street
Boston, MA 02210
(617) 476-5606
606congress.com

Bondir
279A Broadway
Cambridge, MA 02139
(617) 661-0009
bondircambridge.com

Clover Food Lab (Harvard Square location)
7 Holyoke Street
Cambridge, MA 02138
(617) 640-1884
cloverfoodlab.com

Coppa
253 Shawmut Avenue
Boston, MA 02118-2178
(617) 391-0902
coppaboston.com

Cuisine en Locale
Cambridge, MA
(617) 285-0167
enlocale.com

Eat Boston
wheretoeat.in

Erbaluce
69 Church Street
Boston, MA 02116-5418
(617) 426-6969
erbaluce-boston.com

The Gallows
1395 Washington Street
Boston, MA 02118
(617) 425-0200
thegallowsboston.com

Hamersley's Bistro
53 Tremont Street
Boston, MA 02116
(617) 423-2700
hamersleysbistro.com

Henrietta's Table
1 Bennett Street
Cambridge, MA 02138
(617) 661-5005
henriettastable.com

Hungry Mother
233 Cardinal Medeiros Avenue
Cambridge, MA 02141
(617) 499-0090
hungrymothercambridge.com

Island Creek Oyster Bar
500 Commonwealth Avenue
Boston, MA 02215
(617) 532-5300
islandcreekoysterbar.com

L'Espalier
774 Boylston Street
Boston, MA 02199
(617) 262-3023
lespalier.com

Lineage
242 Harvard Street
Brookline, MA 02446
(617) 232-0065
lineagerestaurant.com

Lumiere
1293 Washington Street
Newton, MA 02465
(617) 244-9199
lumiererestaurant.com

Meritage
Boston Harbor Hotel
70 Rowes Wharf
Boston, MA 02110-3300
(617) 439-3995
meritagetherestaurant.com

Nourish
1727 Massachusetts Avenue
Lexington, MA 02420
(781) 674-2400
nourishlexington.com

Oleana
134 Hampshire Street
Cambridge, MA 02139
(617) 661-0505
oleanarestaurant.com

Parsons Table
34 Church Street
Winchester, MA 01890
(617) 729-1040
catchrestaurant.com/parsonstable

Redd's in Rozzie
4257 Washington Street
Roslindale, MA 02131
(617) 325-1000
reddsinrozzie.com

Rendezvous
502 Massachusetts Avenue
Cambridge, MA 02139
(617) 576-1900
rendezvouscentralsquare.com

Rialto
1 Bennett Street
Cambridge, MA 02138
(617) 661-5050
rialto-restaurant.com

Russell House Tavern
14 JFK Street
Cambridge, MA 02138
(617) 500-3055
russellhousecambridge.com

Summer Shack
149 Alewife Brook Parkway
Cambridge, MA 02140
(617) 520-9500
summershackrestaurant.com

Tastings Wine Bar and Bistro
201 Patriot Place
Foxboro, MA 02035
508.203.WINE (9463)
tastingswinebarandbistro.com

Tavolo
1918 Dorchester Avenue
Dorchester Center, MA 02124-3765
(617) 822-1918
tavolopizza.com

Ten Tables
97 Centre Street
Jamaica Plain, MA 02130
(617) 524-8810
tentables.net

Toro
1704 Washington Street
Boston, MA 02118
(617) 536-4300
toro-restaurant.com

Tosca
14 North Street
Hingham, MA 02043
(781) 740-0080
toscahingham.com

TW Food
377 Walden St #A
Cambridge, MA 02138
(617) 864-4745
twfoodrestaurant.com

About the Author and Photographer

Leigh Belanger is a Boston-based food writer and the program director at Chefs Collaborative, a national network of chefs and culinary professionals dedicated to improving the food system through education and community building. She is working on her master's degree in gastronomy from Boston University and is the mother of a very enthusiastic young eater.

Margaret Belanger is a wedding, family, and food photographer based out of Boston. After working on this book, she realized her kitchen is woefully inadequate, as are her cooking skills.

Acknowledgments

From Leigh Belanger:
Many thanks to the people whose work fills this book. I am proud to know the talented, generous group of people who make up Boston's local food community. To the chefs, I can't thank you enough for graciously taking time out of your busy schedules to share your ideas and recipes with me. I learn something every time I talk with one of you. To the farmers and suppliers, you make this region's food worth celebrating. Thanks for the time spent with our team for this book and for your work bringing great food to our tables.

My cousin, Meg Belanger, took the photographs that illustrate these stories. Thanks Meg, for the great eye and the flexibility to fly the plane while we built it. Thanks to Kari Cornell, Melinda Keefe, and the team at Voyageur for working with me on my first book project. Thanks to Ilene Bezhaler for brainstorming ideas with me and for writing the preface. Karoline Boehm-Goodnick, Alexandra Emmott, and Shelby Graham all graciously tracked down hard-to-find ingredients and tested challenging recipes.

To my parents, John and Pat, for the years of support and the hours of babysitting that helped me get through this project, I owe you guys. My brother and my friends listened to me wrestle with the manuscript with humor and honesty. Thanks to Mary and JD, who cheered me on, and to my colleagues at Chefs Collaborative, whose work inspires me to do my best.

Finally, thank you, Galen and Quincy, for making this book better, and for making it possible. I can't tell you how grateful I am to share my life (and my meals) with you both. I love you guys.

From Meg Belanger:
Beef heart. Live clams. Haddock. Whelks. Thank you to all the chefs who shared their time, expertise, and food with me. I never would have tried any of the aforementioned foods if it hadn't been for your enthusiasm. Thanks to the farmers and the fishermen, I have eaten vegetables straight out of the ground, fish right out of the ocean, and meat from animals I met in person. There is no going back now. The idea of trusting the people behind my food hadn't occurred to me before, but now I can't imagine it any other way. You will all be seeing me at your farm stands and restaurants.

Enormous thanks to Leigh for approaching me with this project in the first place! It has been one of the best experiences of my life. You will be hearing from me more than you'd like as I fumble my way through the kitchen trying to cook with all the new ingredients at my disposal.

To Kari and the team at Voyageur Press for presenting me with this awesome opportunity and for being flexible with the inconsistent New England seasons.

To my Auntie Joannie, who is always up for an adventure and knows just how many pairs of latex gloves we'll need to prepare scallops.

To my mom and dad, who always knew I'd end up working on a book, but probably always expected me to be the author and definitely did not think it would have anything to do with food. When I was younger, I made a bet with them that when I was eighteen, I still would not like to eat out. Well, it took a little longer, but I love eating out—especially when chefs like these are preparing the food!

To Doug, for reminding me cooking isn't magic and I can do it too, making his enthusiasm for food contagious (for better or worse), supporting every creative endeavor I embark on, and being my Mr. I love you.

Index

First published in 2012 by Voyageur Press, an imprint of MBI Publishing Company, 400 First Avenue North, Suite 300, Minneapolis, MN 55401 USA

© 2012 Voyageur Press
Text © 2012 Leigh Belanger
Photography © 2012 Margaret Belanger

Voyageur Press titles are also available at discounts in bulk quantity for industrial or sales-promotional use. For details write to Special Sales Manager at MBI Publishing Company, 400 First Avenue North, Suite 300, Minneapolis, MN 55401 USA.

To find out more about our books, visit us online at www.voyageurpress.com.

ISBN-13: 978-0-7603-3908-4

Library of Congress Cataloging-in-Publication Data

Belanger, Leigh, 1974-
The Boston homegrown cookbook : local food, local restaurants, local recipes / Leigh Belanger ; photographs by Margaret Belanger.
    p. cm.
ISBN 978-0-7603-3908-4
1. Cooking, American--New England style. 2. Cooking--Massachusetts--Boston. 3. Cookbooks. I. Title.
TX715.2.N48B45 2012
641.5974--dc23
                           2011030136

Editor: Melinda Keefe
Design Manager: Cindy Samargia Laun
Series Designer: Ellen Huber
Layout: Pauline Molinari

Printed in China

10 9 8 7 6 5 4 3 2 1